The #MeToo Movement

**Recent Title in
21st-Century Turning Points**

The NFL National Anthem Protests
Margaret Haerens

The #MeToo Movement

Laurie Collier Hillstrom

21st-Century Turning Points

An Imprint of ABC-CLIO, LLC
Santa Barbara, California • Denver, Colorado

Library of Congress Cataloging-in-Publication Data

Names: Hillstrom, Laurie Collier, 1965– author.
Title: The #MeToo movement / Laurie Collier Hillstrom.
Description: Santa Barbara, California : ABC-CLIO, [2019] | Series:
    21st-century turning points | Includes bibliographical references and
    index.
Identifiers: LCCN 2018034937 (print) | LCCN 2018038046 (ebook) | ISBN
    9781440867507 (ebook) | ISBN 9781440867491 (hc : alk. paper)
Subjects: LCSH: Sexual abuse victims. | Sex crimes—Prevention. | Sexual
    harassment—Prevention. | Feminism.
Classification: LCC HV6625 (ebook) | LCC HV6625 .H55 2019 (print) | DDC
    362.88—dc23
LC record available at https://lccn.loc.gov/2018034937

ISBN: 978–1–4408–6749–1 (print)
        978–1–4408–6750–7 (ebook)

23 22 21 20 19   1 2 3 4 5

This book is also available as an eBook.

ABC-CLIO
An Imprint of ABC-CLIO, LLC

ABC-CLIO, LLC
130 Cremona Drive, P.O. Box 1911
Santa Barbara, California 93116-1911
www.abc-clio.com

This book is printed on acid-free paper ∞

Manufactured in the United States of America

Contents

Series Foreword

21st-Century Turning Points is a general reference series that has been crafted for use by high school and undergraduate students as well as members of the general public. The purpose of the series is to give readers a clear, authoritative, and unbiased understanding of major fast-breaking events, movements, people, and issues that are transforming American life, culture, and politics in this turbulent new century. Each volume constitutes a one-stop resource for learning about a single issue or event currently dominating America's news headlines and political discussions—issues or events that, in many cases, are also driving national debate about our country's leaders, institutions, values, and priorities.

Each volume in the *21st-Century Turning Points* series begins with an **Overview** of the event or issue that is the subject of the book. It then provides a suite of informative chronologically arranged narrative entries on specific **Landmarks** in the evolution of the event or issue in question. This section provides both vital historical context and insights into present-day news events to give readers a full and clear understanding of how current issues and controversies evolved.

The next section of the book is devoted to examining the **Impacts** of the event or issue in question on various aspects of American life, including political, economic, cultural, and interpersonal implications. It is followed by a chapter of biographical **Profiles** that summarize the life experiences and personal beliefs of prominent individuals associated with the event or issue in question.

Finally, each book concludes with a topically organized **Further Resources** list of important and informative resources—from influential books to fascinating websites—to which readers can turn for additional information, and a carefully compiled subject **Index**.

These complementary elements, found in every book in the series, work together to create an evenhanded, authoritative, and user-friendly tool for gaining a deeper and more accurate understanding of the fast-changing nation in which we live—and the issues and moments that define us as we move deeper into the twenty-first century.

CHAPTER ONE

Overview of the #MeToo Movement

"Me too."

By posting these two words on social media, millions of women established a community of survivors and launched a social change movement to end sexual harassment and assault. Activist Tarana Burke first recognized the power of the words a decade earlier, when she used them to offer solace, support, and solidarity to a young girl who entrusted her with a report of sexual abuse. The words gained new relevance in October 2017, when dozens of female celebrities came forward to accuse Hollywood producer Harvey Weinstein of sexual misconduct. In the wake of the Weinstein scandal, actress Alyssa Milano invited people who had experienced sexual harassment or assault to use the words to demonstrate the pervasiveness of the problem. Her request received an overwhelming response, as women around the world shared their stories on social media using the hashtag #MeToo. "A basic concept of #MeToo is the power of numbers across time: the difference between a single victim, whose lone account might not be believed, and the choruses of 'me too' that make each individual's account that much more believable," wrote Jeannie Suk Gersen in the *New Yorker*. "When it comes down to it, #MeToo itself constitutes an evidentiary claim of sorts: what you say happened to you happened to me, too, and so it is more likely that we are both telling the truth" (Gersen 2018).

Research confirmed the anecdotal evidence offered by the #MeToo social media campaign. A 2018 survey by the nonprofit organization Stop Street Harassment found that 81 percent of women in the United States had experienced some form of sexual harassment, ranging from whistles and catcalls to leering, stalking, groping, and sexual assault. More than half of women reported being touched in a sexual manner without their permission, while

27 percent reported being victims of sexual assault. Two-thirds of women experienced sexual harassment in public spaces, and 38 percent experienced it in the workplace. Only 10 percent of women reported the harassment to an authority figure, while less than 1 percent confronted the perpetrator. Instead, most women responded to sexual harassment by making changes in their own lives and daily routines, such as quitting a job, stopping an activity, switching schools, or moving to a new residence (Chatterjeee 2018).

Misogyny and Feminism

Some analysts view sexual harassment as a manifestation of systemic misogyny in American society. They contend that misogyny—characterized by contempt, hostility, denigration, objectification, and violence aimed at women—served as an organizing principle throughout U.S. history and is still reflected in a patriarchal system of male dominance and female subordination in politics, business, and popular culture. As evidence of the historical devaluation of women in the United States, they point to the fact that only 52 women have served in the U.S. Senate during its first 230 years in existence. In addition, they note that working women today earn an average of 80 cents for every dollar paid to men, and that female executives lead less than 5 percent of *Fortune* 500 companies.

According to management consultant Michelle Kim, this gender-based power structure—combined with ingrained attitudes of entitlement and privilege among men—creates an environment where gender discrimination and sexual harassment can thrive. "Our entire society is built on systems of patriarchy, toxic masculinity, and rape culture," she wrote. "The ways in which we shame, blame, and doubt survivors of sexual violence ('what were you wearing?' 'are you sure that's what happened?' 'were you drunk?'), how our legal systems are built to center the needs of perpetrators, and how early education around sexual violence focuses on reactionary caution ('buy your own drink,' 'don't walk alone at night,' 'cover your skin') … these are all examples of how we subconsciously and consciously perpetuate the cycle of gender-based violence in our society" (Kim 2017).

Feminism arose to counteract the forces of misogyny in American culture. Historians have identified several key feminist movements or waves—including the women's suffrage movement of the nineteenth and early twentieth centuries and the women's liberation movement of the 1960s and 1970s—that made significant strides toward attaining political and social equality for American women. Women gained voting rights with the 1920 passage of the Nineteenth Amendment, for instance, and they achieved reproductive freedom through a series of landmark Supreme Court cases. The inclusion of "sex" as a protected category in the Civil Rights Act of 1964 outlawed discrimination on the basis of gender. The Equal Employment Opportunity Commission (EEOC) used Title VII of the Civil Rights Act as the basis of its 1980 rules prohibiting sexual harassment in the workplace.

Attorney Anita Hill helped launch another wave of feminist activism in 1991 with her appearance at the confirmation hearings for Supreme Court nominee Clarence Thomas. In televised testimony that riveted the nation, Hill claimed that Thomas had subjected her to a pattern of inappropriate remarks and offensive conduct when she worked for him a decade earlier. Thomas emphatically denied Hill's accusations, calling them politically motivated. Hill's shocking allegations raised public awareness of workplace sexual harassment and empowered more women to come forward, resulting in a record number of complaints filed with the EEOC. The skeptical interrogation she endured from members of the all-male Senate Judiciary Committee, meanwhile, generated outrage and resentment among many women. Determined to change the atmosphere in politics, a record number of women ran for office in 1992, which became known as the "Year of the Woman."

Some observers place the #MeToo movement within this broader context of American feminism and view it as another historic milestone in the fight for women's rights. "To the extent that women's bodies are still treated as public property by men, whether that means groping us or deciding what we can do with our uteruses, women do not have civic equality," Laura Kipnis wrote in the *Guardian*. "To miss that point is to miss the political importance and the political lineage of #MeToo: the latest step in a centuries long political struggle for women to simply control our own bodies" (Kipnis 2018).

A key factor differentiating the #MeToo movement from its predecessors—and amplifying its impact—is activists' extensive use of social media tools. Since Milano's tweet first popularized the #MeToo hashtag on Twitter, supporters have used online platforms to share information, plan and organize protest actions, propagate political messages, and debate feminist ideas. Some activists have also used social media to expose sexual harassment by individuals and within institutions. Software engineer Susan Fowler, for instance, recounted her work experience at Uber in a viral blog post that revealed a pervasive culture of sexual harassment in the technology industry. Fowler's post also prompted an internal investigation that ultimately led to the resignation of Uber's founder. "It has given a voice to many, like myself, who otherwise wouldn't have had a platform," Fowler said of social media. "#MeToo is a perfect example.... It made the rest of the world finally understand the true extent of inappropriate behavior against women, and the damage it causes" (Hook 2017).

#MeToo and Women's Empowerment

Many social commentators have argued that the 2016 presidential campaign served as a precipitating factor in the development of the #MeToo movement. The campaign featured the first female presidential nominee from a major political party, Democrat Hillary Clinton. Her candidacy brought issues of gender equality and sexism to the forefront of American politics. Critics accused her opponent, Republican Donald Trump, of making misogynistic remarks throughout his campaign. Trump claimed that a female journalist questioned him aggressively because she was menstruating, for instance, and he implied that a female political rival was not attractive enough to hold office. Shortly before the November election, a recording surfaced in which Trump seemingly boasted about taking advantage of his celebrity to commit sexual assault. Several women subsequently came forward to accuse Trump of sexual misconduct, but his supporters either did not believe the allegations or felt they did not disqualify him from becoming president.

When voters went to the polls, many feminists harbored strong hopes that the United States would elect its first female president. They responded to Trump's electoral victory with grief and outrage. Critics expressed concern that his leadership on the world stage would normalize misogyny and reverse gains toward women's equality. In January 2017, one day after Trump's inauguration, more than 3 million people in 400 cities and towns across the United States expressed their determination to stand up for women's rights by participating in the Women's March. "A lot of people started off this year feeling a sense of hopelessness, because we had a president in our office who was self-admitted to be a sexual predator," #MeToo founder Tarana Burke acknowledged. "As a woman, as an American citizen, that is disheartening to know that the person who is the leader of your country thinks like that and operates like that.... In ways I think that it has emboldened women and empowered us to step up and amplify our voices even louder" (Snyder and Lopez 2017).

The sense of empowerment generated by the Women's March, coupled with the public debate over Trump's alleged sexual misconduct, prompted several women to come forward with accusations against other men in positions of power in early 2017. Fowler's blog post appeared in February, for instance, and Fox News fired host Bill O'Reilly in April after multiple women accused him of sexual harassment. The turning point in breaking the silence came in October of that year, however, when *New York Times* investigative journalists Jodi Kantor and Megan Twohey published an article detailing allegations of sexual misconduct—ranging from unwelcome advances to rape—against Weinstein spanning his 30-year career as one of the most successful producers in Hollywood. His accusers eventually included dozens of film stars, such as Ashley Judd, Gwyneth Paltrow, Angelina Jolie, Uma Thurman, Lupita Nyong'o, and Salma Hayek.

The Weinstein scandal opened the floodgates of #MeToo disclosures. After Milano introduced the hashtag on Twitter, it appeared in 2.3 million tweets by users in 85 different countries within a matter of weeks (Fox and Diehm 2017). Over the next few months, more than 200 prominent men in various fields faced allegations of sexual misconduct. In the atmosphere of reduced tolerance created by the #MeToo campaign, many of the accused men suddenly found their reputations ruined and their careers ended. "There is a kind of unmasking going on," said Robin Lakoff, a professor at the University of California at Berkeley. "A lot of these are people who are venerated, people who were taken very seriously" (Hook 2017). Seeking to sustain the momentum, #MeToo activists launched Time's Up, a series of initiatives aimed at helping working women fight sexual harassment and lobbying for legislative changes to hold perpetrators accountable.

Criticism and Backlash

During the last few months of 2017, every day seemed to bring new media reports about powerful men being accused of sexual misconduct. The flurry of allegations and repercussions raised concerns about potential negative effects of the #MeToo reckoning. Some critics characterized #MeToo activists as dangerous extremists who rushed to judgment and denied due process in their zeal to destroy men. "They believe they are fighting an insidious, ubiquitous evil—the patriarchy—just as the extreme anti-Communists in the 1950s believed that commies were everywhere and so foul they didn't deserve a presumption of innocence, or simple human decency," columnist Andrew Sullivan argued. "They demand public confessions of the guilty and public support for their cause … or they will cast suspicion on you as well" (Sullivan 2018). Other critics worried that #MeToo activists could harm the feminist cause by publicizing unsubstantiated allegations.

Some of the #MeToo backlash focused on the movement's impact on relationships between men and women, whether professional relationships in the workplace or personal relationships on the dating scene. Critics contended that the avalanche of high-profile allegations created an atmosphere of fear, mistrust, and confusion, as men struggled to understand the new standards of appropriate behavior toward women. They warned that men's feelings of discomfort could result in fewer job opportunities for women. "Many men will absorb the lessons of late 2017 to be not about the threat they've posed to women but about the threat that women pose to them," journalist Rebecca Traister stated. "So there will be more—perhaps unconscious—hesitancy about hiring women, less eagerness to invite them to lunch, or send them on work trips with men; men will be warier of mentoring women" (Traister 2017).

Some critics charged that the #MeToo disclosures often failed to differentiate between conduct that merely made women feel uncomfortable—such as unwelcome flirtation—and sexual violence. They argued that zero tolerance policies, which required perpetrators to be punished regardless of the level of offense, portrayed women as helpless victims who were incapable of protecting their own interests. "Why would you need such stringent rules unless you view women as essentially weak creatures who can't stand up for themselves?" journalist Heather Wilhelm wrote. "It's strangely Victorian. It's also pretty darn anti-feminist, as far as I can see. Strangely, modern feminism seems to have shifted our cultural focus from supposed 'empowerment' and 'choice' to treating people like not-so-resourceful children" (Wilhelm 2018).

#MeToo supporters, on the other hand, argue that the movement has brought much-needed public attention to the pervasiveness of sexual harassment and assault. They view it as a long-overdue reckoning that shed light on forms of degradation and abuse that women had always silently endured in order to keep their jobs, or secretly warned each other about through "whisper networks," or reluctantly altered their lives to avoid. They marvel at the fact that two words empowered women around the world to join together and speak out against sexism, misogyny, and discrimination. "We should not mourn the end of the creative lives of the men being outed as predators; we should contemplate the creative contributions we never had, will never know, because their creators were crushed or shut out," said writer Rebecca Solnit. "The losses due to misogyny and racism have been normalized forever. The task has been to de-normalize them and break the silence they impose. To make a society in which everyone's story gets told" (Solnit 2017).

Further Reading

Chatterjeee, Rhitu. 2018. "A New Survey Finds 81% of Women Have Experienced Sexual Harassment." NPR, February 21. https://www.npr.org/sections/thetwo-way/2018/02/21/587671849/a-new-survey-finds-eighty-percent-of-women-have-experienced-sexual-harassment

Fox, Kara, and Jan Diehm. 2017. "#MeToo's Global Moment: Anatomy of a Viral Campaign." CNN, November 9. https://www.cnn.com/2017/11/09/world/metoo-hashtag-global-movement/index.html

Gersen, Jeannie S. 2018. "Bill Cosby's Crimes and the Impact of #MeToo on the American Legal System." *New Yorker*, April 27. https://www.newyorker.com/news/news-desk/bill-cosbys-crimes-and-the-impact-of-metoo-on-the-american-legal-system

Hook, Leslie. 2017. "FT Person of the Year: Susan Fowler." *Financial Times*, December 11. https://www.ft.com/content/b4bc2a68-dc4f-11e7-a039-c64b1c09b482

Kim, Michelle. 2017. "How Companies Can Respond to the #MeToo Movement." *Medium*, October 30. https://medium.com/awaken-blog/how-companies-can-respond-to-the-metoo-movement-8b5d22bef9ae

Kipnis, Laura. 2018. "Has #MeToo Gone Too Far, or Not Far Enough? The Answer Is Both." *Guardian*, January 13. https://www.theguardian.com/commentisfree/2018/jan/13/has-me-too-catherine-deneuve-laura-kipnis

Snyder, Chris, and Linette Lopez. 2017. "The Woman behind the #MeToo Movement on Why She Would Never Meet with Trump." *Business Insider*, December 7. http://www.businessinsider.com/metoo-movement-founder-tarana-burke-donald-trump-time-person-of-year-2017-12

Solnit, Rebecca. 2017. "Let This Flood of Women's Stories Never Cease." *Literary Hub*, November 14. https://lithub.com/rebecca-solnit-let-this-flood-of-womens-stories-never-cease/

Sullivan, Andrew. 2018. "It's Time to Resist the Excesses of #MeToo." *New York Magazine*, January 12. http://nymag.com/daily/intelligencer/2018/01/andrew-sullivan-time-to-resist-excesses-of-metoo.html

Traister, Rebecca. 2017. "Your Reckoning. And Mine." *Cut*, November 12. https://www.thecut.com/2017/11/rebecca-traister-on-the-post-weinstein-reckoning.html

Wilhelm, Heather. 2018. "The Awkward Side Effects of #MeToo." *Chicago Tribune*, February 12. http://www.chicagotribune.com/news/opinion/commentary/ct-perspec-wilhelm-me-too-google-facebook-dating-0212-story.html

CHAPTER TWO

Landmark Events

This section explores important milestones and events in the evolution of the #MeToo movement, from the coining of the term "sexual harassment" during the feminist movement of the 1970s to the Harvey Weinstein scandal of 2017 and subsequent revelations of sexual misconduct in American news, politics, entertainment, and business.

Title VII of the Civil Rights Act Prohibits Sex Discrimination (1964)

Discrimination against women was legal throughout most of U.S. history. Beginning during the colonial era, members of the so-called weaker sex were not allowed to vote, hold public office, or serve on a jury. Women's rights were subordinate to those of their husbands, fathers, or brothers with regard to property ownership, inheritance, and contracts. The Declaration of Independence explicitly noted that "all men are created equal," while the U.S. Constitution failed to codify women's equality by only referring to "persons," who were interpreted as being male under British common law.

One early effort to generate support for gender equality came in 1848, when a group of 300 prominent female abolitionists gathered at the Seneca Falls Convention in New York. The meeting produced a set of resolutions that called for granting women greater social, religious, and civil rights, including the right to vote. It took seven decades, however, before American women gained voting rights nationwide with the ratification of the Nineteenth Amendment in 1920. Three years later, suffrage activist Alice Paul (1885–1977) drafted the Equal Rights Amendment (ERA), which would formally prohibit discrimination on the basis of sex in the United States. Although the ERA was introduced repeatedly in Congress, it took five decades before the measure finally passed in 1972, and the amendment stalled out before being ratified by the required number of states.

In the meantime, American women continued to face discrimination—particularly in the realm of employment—through the early 1960s. Men were widely viewed as the head of the household and the primary bread-winner. Many employers offered men preferential access to jobs based on the belief that they needed income to support their families. Employers only considered women for certain jobs, such as secretaries, waitresses, sales clerks, housekeepers, nurses, and teachers. Even in these traditionally "female" occupations, women faced societal expectations to quit working once they got married in order to become housewives and mothers.

Women were denied jobs in many fields, especially those that involved physical labor, and labor unions excluded women from membership. Many state laws sought to "protect" female employees by restricting their working hours. Classified employment advertisements in newspapers of the era featured separate listings for male and female workers. Commercial airlines hired female flight attendants on the basis of their physical attractiveness and fired them if their appearance changed. Many other companies refused to hire women who had young children and fired female employees when they got married or became pregnant.

Women also routinely received less pay than men for the same work. The Equal Pay Act of 1963, signed into law by President John F. Kennedy (1917–1963), sought to address gender-based wage discrimination by prohibiting employers from paying female employees a lower rate than male employees for jobs that were performed under similar conditions and required substantially equal skill, effort, and responsibility. The law made exceptions for pay differentials imposed on a basis other than gender, such as seniority, merit, or production quantity.

Extending Civil Rights Protections to Women

Despite the passage of the Equal Pay Act, most Americans viewed women's rights as secondary in the early 1960s. The civil rights movement shone a spotlight on the insidious problem of racial segregation with a series of sit-ins, freedom rides, and protest marches that often faced violent repression. With input from the Reverend Martin Luther King Jr. (1929–1968) and other black leaders, the Kennedy administration drafted strong new civil rights legislation that would prohibit racial discrimination in employment, education, and private businesses that served the public. After Kennedy's assassination, President Lyndon B. Johnson (1908–1973) promoted passage of the bill as a means of honoring his predecessor's legacy.

The proposed legislation met with staunch resistance from Southern Democrats in Congress. While the House of Representatives debated the bill, Democrat Howard W. Smith (1883–1976) of Virginia introduced an amendment that added the word "sex" to the designated bases on which citizens would be afforded protection from employment discrimination, along with race, color, religion, and national origin. Since Smith vocally opposed civil rights, his colleagues assumed that he intended for the amendment to serve as a "poison pill" that would help derail the bill's passage. The idea of women's equality seemed so absurd to other congressmen that Smith's request prompted laughter and jokes on the House floor. Smith later claimed, however, that he offered the amendment at the behest of Alice Paul and other activists in a genuine effort to protect women's rights.

Regardless of his true motivations, Smith's maneuver incensed civil rights advocates, many of whom opposed extending the legislation's protections to women. Some black leaders felt that doing so would trivialize the long, bloody struggle to end racial segregation. Others downplayed the discrimination faced by women or argued that their concerns were too different from those of African Americans to cover in a single piece of legislation. Some critics worried that the controversial addition of "sex" would alienate liberal allies in Congress and break up the fragile coalition of supporters needed to ensure the legislation's passage. They insisted that women's rights should wait until black civil rights had been secured.

Representative Martha W. Griffiths (1912–2003), a Democrat from Michigan, emerged as the most eloquent defender of Smith's amendment. She argued that her colleagues' ridicule of the notion of women's equality proved that legal protections were needed. She also pointed out that passing the bill without adding "sex" would leave white women with fewer rights than black women. In the end, the House passed a version of the bill that prohibited sex discrimination. The legislation faced even tougher opposition in the Senate, where Southern Democrats staged a 60-day filibuster before Republican Everett M. Dirksen (1896–1969) of Illinois finally rounded up enough support to force a vote. Johnson signed the Civil Rights Act of 1964 into law on July 2. The landmark legislation, which has been called "the bill of the century" (Risen 2014), ended racial segregation in the United States and extended full civil rights protections to African Americans.

Title VII of the law has also proven instrumental in protecting women from discrimination in the workplace. It prohibits employers from discriminating on the basis of race, color, religion, sex, or national origin in decisions related to hiring, compensation, training, promotion, or firing of employees, as well as in the terms and conditions of employment. One historian noted that Griffiths, Smith, and Paul "gave women the handle to the door to economic opportunity, and nearly all the gains women have made in that sphere since the 1960s were made because of what they did" (Menand 2014).

Title VII also created the Equal Employment Opportunity Commission (EEOC) to enforce the law. The first chairman of the agency, Franklin D. Roosevelt Jr. (1914–1988), openly dismissed the idea of equal rights for women in the workplace and refused to enforce the law's provisions against sex discrimination. In response to a reporter who inquired, "What about sex?" Roosevelt quipped, "I'm all for it" (Thomas 2016, p. 4). In 1966, women's rights activists formed the National Organization for Women (NOW), an advocacy group that pushed for vigorous enforcement of Title VII. The U.S. Supreme Court heard its first gender-discrimination case under the law in 1971. Its unanimous decision in *Phillips v. Martin Marietta* found that the employer's policy against hiring women with young children violated the Civil Rights Act.

Debating the Fairness of Affirmative Action

The role of the EEOC has grown over time to include investigating complaints, enforcing laws, and conducting educational programs related to employment discrimination. Later laws and amendments expanded the designated bases for protection under Title VII to include age, disability, and genetic information. Legislation and court decisions also expanded the concept of sex discrimination to include pregnancy, childbirth, gender identity, and sexual orientation. The EEOC received 25,600 charges of sex discrimination in 2017, accounting for 30 percent of all charges filed with the agency, as well as nearly 6,700 charges of sexual harassment (EEOC 2018).

Perhaps the most controversial aspect of the EEOC's mandate to address discrimination is the concept of affirmative action. Although the text of the Civil Rights Act did not use that terminology, the law gave the EEOC broad authority to create rules and programs to promote equal employment opportunity for all people, regardless of race, sex, or other characteristics. At times, these rules and programs have featured positive actions designed to remedy past discrimination and affirmatively protect the civil rights of designated classes of citizens. Affirmative action policies also have been promoted by executive orders, court decisions, and federal and state regulations.

As the agency charged with implementing and enforcing these policies, the EEOC has generated considerable controversy. Opponents of affirmative action argue that such measures are unfair, because they tend to advance the employment opportunities available to some citizens by limiting those available to other citizens—specifically, to white male citizens. Critics refer to this situation as "reverse discrimination," and they view it as an example of excessive government interference in business and the economy. Advocates of affirmative action, on the other hand, portray it as a valuable tool to help historically disadvantaged groups achieve equality.

Further Reading

Equal Employment Opportunity Commission. 2018. "EEOC Releases Fiscal Year 2017 Enforcement and Litigation Data." https://www.eeoc.gov/eeoc/statistics/enforcement/index.cfm

Menand, Louis. 2014. "The Sex Amendment: How Women Got in on the Civil Rights Act." *New Yorker*, July 21. https://www.newyorker.com/magazine/2014/07/21/sex-amendment

Purdum, Todd S. 2014. *An Idea Whose Time Has Come: Two Presidents, Two Parties, and the Battle for the Civil Rights Act of 1964.* New York: Macmillan.

Risen, Clay. 2014. *The Bill of the Century: The Epic Battle for the Civil Rights Act.* New York: Bloomsbury.

Simmons, Linda. 2018. "The Civil Rights Act of 1964 and the Equal Opportunity Employment Commission." *National Archives and Records Administration.* https://www.archives.gov/education/lessons/civil-rights-act

Thomas, Gillian. 2016. *Because of Sex: One Law, Ten Cases, and Fifty Years That Changed American Women's Lives at Work.* New York: Picador.

Sexual Harassment Enters the Lexicon (1975)

Title VII of the Civil Rights Act of 1964 removed many barriers to equal participation in the workforce for American women. By prohibiting discrimination on the basis of sex in employment practices, it opened the door to new job opportunities. The percentage of women in professional positions nearly doubled within a few years of the law's passage, from 14 percent in 1966 to 27 percent in 1972 (EEOC 2014). As women's participation in the workforce grew, however, so did the number of women who experienced mistreatment on the job in the form of predatory sexual behavior by male supervisors, foremen, managers, and coworkers.

In offices, factories, shops, restaurants, and other places of employment across the country, female workers were often subjected to sexual innuendo and lewd gestures, pinching and groping, or propositions and coercion during the late 1960s and early 1970s. Male dominance and female subordination characterized the gender dynamic in a typical workplace. Some male bosses leveraged their status to take liberties with their female employees. Many working women came to view fending off unwanted sexual advances as an unfortunate, but inevitable, part of their jobs. Most victims resigned themselves to the situation and silently endured insults and indignities for the sake of their careers. When women complained, their concerns were rarely taken seriously. Most men in managerial positions dismissed such behavior as harmless and advised female employees to quit if it bothered them.

This situation began to change with the rise of the women's liberation movement in the late 1960s. The National Organization for Women (NOW), founded in 1966 by feminist author Betty Friedan (1921–2006), fought for vigorous enforcement of Title VII to achieve gender equality in the workplace. More radical elements of the movement rejected symbols of women's confinement to traditional gender roles by burning bras, eschewing makeup, and discarding pots and pans. Women's rights activists disrupted the 1968 Miss America Pageant, which they viewed as contributing to the objectification of women, and thousands of feminists took a day off from domestic responsibilities to participate in the 1970 Women's Strike for Equality.

The women's liberation movement achieved some notable successes in the early 1970s. In 1972, Congress finally passed the Equal Rights Amendment, which women's suffrage activists originally drafted 50 years earlier. Lawmakers also adopted Title IX, a wide-reaching civil rights amendment that prohibited sex discrimination in public education, including athletics. In 1973, the Supreme Court issued its landmark ruling in *Roe v. Wade*, which legalized abortion in the United States. Recognizing these advances, *Time* magazine bestowed its 1975 Man of the Year honor on "American women."

Coining the Term "Sexual Harassment"

This atmosphere of change and empowerment encouraged a growing number of women to speak out about the pervasive problem of predatory sexual behavior in the workplace. One such woman was Carmita Wood, a 44-year-old mother of four who began working as an administrative assistant in the physics department at Cornell University in the late 1960s. Her supervisor was the renowned nuclear physicist Boyce McDaniel (1917–2002), who served as director of Cornell's Laboratory of Nuclear Sciences. Wood accused McDaniel of leering at her, making inappropriate remarks to her, groping her, and kissing her without permission. Although she requested a transfer to a different department, Cornell administrators refused to grant her request. The abuse continued throughout her eight years of employment at the university, and the stressful situation took a severe toll on her physical and mental health. Wood's desperation grew until she was finally forced to quit her job in 1974. She then filed for unemployment benefits, but Cornell denied her claim because she had voluntarily terminated her employment for reasons it deemed "personal and non-compelling" (Mearhoff 2018).

In 1975, Wood told her story to Lin Farley (1942–), a feminist who worked in Cornell's Human Affairs Office and taught a field-study course at the university called Women and Work. Farley had heard countless similar tales from female students, who often used her class as a forum to discuss predatory sexual behavior that had made them feel uncomfortable, degraded, or intimidated in the workplace. Farley organized a meeting with several colleagues to develop a plan for challenging this situation. The first step, they decided, was to coin a term to describe the problem succinctly. "I thought that we needed to have a name for what this phenomenon was," Farley explained. "It was something that we all talked about, but because we didn't have a name, we didn't know we were all talking about the same thing" (Gladstone 2017). They settled upon the term "sexual harassment."

Farley and her colleagues formed a group called Working Women United to combat sexual harassment in the workplace. The group organized a "speak out" event that attracted nearly 300 participants from the surrounding community. University employees, factory workers, secretaries, and waitresses all related similar experiences of sexual harassment on the job, with offensive practices ranging from pats on the rear end to forceful demands for sexual favors. A survey of attendees revealed that more than 70 percent had experienced sexual harassment personally, while 92 percent agreed that it was a serious problem (Nemy 1975).

Sexual harassment entered the lexicon in August 1975, after Farley used the term while testifying at a hearing about women in the workplace convened by the Commission on Human Rights of New York City. "Sexual harassment of women in their place of employment is extremely widespread," she declared. "It is literally epidemic" (Nemy 1975). After describing the various forms of torment that women commonly encountered on the job, Farley argued that sexual harassment violated workers' civil rights and human dignity. The *New York Times* published an article about the hearing that included the term "sexual harassment" in its headline. Newspapers across the country reprinted the story, helping raise public awareness and spark a national conversation about the issue.

Codifying Sexual Harassment as an Offense

Public exposure of the long-hidden problem of sexual harassment had a profound impact on the lives of working women in America. By giving the phenomenon a name and revealing its ubiquitous nature, Farley and her colleagues at Cornell validated the experiences of millions of women and let them know they were not alone. Women's rights activists launched a campaign to stamp out sexual harassment and help women who were victimized by it achieve legal redress.

In her seminal 1979 book *Sexual Harassment of Working Women*, feminist attorney Catharine A. MacKinnon (1946–) outlined a legal theory of sexual harassment that included two categories of offense: persistent practices that create a hostile working environment for women, and quid pro quo arrangements that require sexual compliance in exchange for employment opportunity or career advancement. The following year, the Equal Opportunity Employment Commission (EEOC) ruled that these two forms of sexual harassment constituted sex discrimination, which allowed women to sue their employers under Title VII. After decades of mistreating female employees with impunity, male bosses finally began to face consequences for engaging in sexual harassment.

The intense public focus on sexual harassment prompted a conservative backlash in the late 1970s and early 1980s. Confronted with an increasing number of accusations and lawsuits, some critics portrayed sexual harassment complaints as an example of women's liberation run amuck. They claimed that women workers were oversensitive, or misinterpreted men's intentions, or should be flattered by male attention. In testimony before a Senate committee examining federal policy on sexual harassment in the workplace, conservative activist Phyllis Schlafly (1924–2016) blamed the problem on suggestive dress or behavior by female employees, asserting that "virtuous women are seldom accosted" (Cohen 2016).

In the meantime, Cornell responded to the initial revelations of sexual harassment by establishing one of the nation's first women's studies departments and becoming a leader in academic research on sex discrimination. Although the university never awarded unemployment compensation to Wood, it did give her a new job in a different department. Farley emerged as a leading expert on sexual harassment who provided corporate consulting and management training services to help businesses protect their employees from unwanted sexual advances in the workplace.

Further Reading

Cohen, Sascha. 2016. "A Brief History of Sexual Harassment in America before Anita Hill." *Time*, April 11. http://time.com/4286575/sexual-harassment -before-anita-hill/

Equal Employment Opportunity Commission. 2014. "Women in the American Workforce." https://www.eeoc.gov/eeoc/statistics/reports/american_experiences/women.cfm

Gladstone, Brooke. 2017. "Sexual Harassment, Revisited." *On the Media*, WNYC, October 21. https://www.wnyc.org/story/sexual-harassment-revisited/?tab=transcript

MacKinnon, Catharine A. 1979. *Sexual Harassment of Working Women*. New Haven, CT: Yale University Press.

Mearhoff, Sarah. 2018. "#MeToo: Fight against Workplace Sexual Harassment Began at Cornell in 1975." *Ithaca Journal*, February 21. https://www.ithacajournal.com/story/news/local/2018/02/21/metoo-fight-against-workplace-sexual-harassment-began-cornell-1975/347388002/

Nemy, Enid. 1975. "Women Begin to Speak Out against Sexual Harassment at Work." *New York Times*, August 19. https://www.nytimes.com/1975/08/19/archives/women-begin-to-speak-out-against-sexual-harassment-at-work.html

The EEOC Issues Guidelines on Sexual Harassment (1980)

When feminists at Cornell University coined the term "sexual harassment" in 1975, they gave American women a common vocabulary to discuss the predatory sexual behavior that many of them endured in the workplace. Emboldened by the realization that they were not alone in their experiences, an increasing number of female employees refused to tolerate sexual harassment and began filing claims with the Equal Employment Opportunity Commission (EEOC).

Initial court rulings, though, raised questions as to whether victims of sexual harassment could hold their employers liable for the mistreatment they experienced in the workplace. Even though Title VII of the Civil Rights Act of 1964 outlawed employment discrimination on the basis of sex, most cases litigated in the decade after its passage focused on challenging employer policies that treated male and female workers differently with regard to hiring, wages, promotions, benefits, or terms of employment. Since no employers had formal policies condoning the sexual harassment of employees, many legal scholars argued that Title VII protections did not apply to the practice.

Although a growing number of Americans viewed sexual harassment in the workplace as unfair or reprehensible, they also tended to think of it as an interpersonal problem rather than a legal issue. They regarded sexuality as a private matter that was not related to the employment context, and thus not covered by employment law. They envisioned sexual harassment as an isolated action by an individual employee seeking to satisfy a personal desire, urge, or proclivity. Since the employee's misconduct was not sanctioned by the employer and did not serve a legitimate business interest, they claimed that the employer should not be held legally liable for it.

Early court decisions in sexual harassment cases adopted this view. In the 1975 case of *Corne v. Bausch and Lomb*, 390 F. Supp. 161 (D. Ariz. 1975), for instance, a U.S. District Court judge said it was "ludicrous" to define a supervisor's unwanted sexual advances toward two female employees as sex discrimination under federal civil rights law. "An outgrowth of holding such activity to be actionable under Title VII would be a potential federal lawsuit every time any employee made amorous or sexually oriented advances toward another," the opinion stated. "The only sure way an employer could avoid such charges would be to have employees who were asexual."

Feminists continued pushing for a new legal interpretation of sexual harassment in the workplace. They argued that it should qualify as sex discrimination because victims' status as women was a determining factor in its occurrence. They also contended that it violated women's civil rights by denying them equal opportunity to perform their jobs. "Sexual harassment exemplifies and promotes employment practices which disadvantage women in work and sexual practices which intimately degrade and objectify women," feminist attorney Catharine A. MacKinnon (1946–) wrote in her seminal 1979 book *Sexual Harassment of Working Women*. "In the broader perspective, sexual harassment at work undercuts women's potential for social equality in two interpenetrated ways: by using her employment position to coerce her sexually, while using her sexual position to coerce her economically" (p. 7).

Federal courts slowly began applying this theory. In the 1977 case of *Barnes v. Costle*, 561 F. 2d 983, for instance, the U.S. Circuit Court of Appeals for the District of Columbia found that sexual harassment constituted sex discrimination when a male supervisor used the power of his employment position to impose conditions on a female employee in the workplace. "But for her womanhood, her participation in sexual activity would never have been solicited," the ruling noted. "She became the target of her superior's sexual desires because she was a woman, and was asked to bow to his demands as the price for holding her job." Sexual advances by a person with supervisory authority that were connected to employment-related decisions—such as whether to promote or fire an employee—became known as "quid pro quo" sexual harassment.

The EEOC Clarifies and Expands Sexual Harassment Rules

The EEOC, which had been created under the Civil Rights Act of 1964 to enforce federal antidiscrimination statutes, finally weighed in on sexual harassment in 1980. Eleanor Holmes Norton (1937–), a noted civil rights activist and lawyer, headed the agency at that time. She became the first female EEOC chair when President Jimmy Carter (1924–) appointed her three years earlier. After convening a series of hearings on sex discrimination in the workplace, Norton issued the first EEOC guidelines on sexual harassment, which formally recognized it as a form of sex discrimination prohibited under Title VII.

The EEOC guidelines provided the following definition of sexual harassment:

> Unwelcome sexual advances, requests for sexual favors, and other verbal or physical conduct of a sexual nature constitute sexual harassment when 1) submission to such conduct is made either explicitly or implicitly a term or condition of an individual's employment, 2) submission to or rejection of such conduct by an individual is used as the basis for employment decisions affecting such individual, or 3) such conduct has the purpose or effect of unreasonably interfering with an individual's work performance or creating an intimidating, hostile, or offensive working environment. (EEOC 1990)

The new EEOC rules did not prohibit all sexual conduct in workplace settings—only "unwelcome" sexual conduct that affected the conditions of an individual's employment. The guidelines formally prohibited "quid pro quo" arrangements, which the courts had already established as a form of sex discrimination. They also broadened the legal definition of sexual harassment to include conduct by coworkers that created a "hostile working environment." Conduct that created a sexually charged atmosphere in the workplace might include making suggestive remarks, telling offensive jokes, or displaying explicit materials. The EEOC recognized such conduct as sex discrimination because persistent exposure to it had the potential to affect the conditions of employment and cause psychological harm. Employers could be held liable for a hostile work environment if management knew or should have known about the situation.

Challenges to the EEOC Sexual Harassment Policy

Shortly after the EEOC introduced its new sexual harassment guidelines, Republican Ronald Reagan (1911–2004) was elected president of the United States. As a leading proponent of conservative "family values," Reagan opposed the Equal Rights Amendment, abortion rights, and other feminist priorities. In 1981, the Senate Labor Committee convened hearings to evaluate the EEOC's proposed sexual harassment policies. Republican Senator Orrin Hatch (1934–) of Utah argued that the new regulations were intrusive and unnecessary. He claimed the regulations would burden the U.S. economy rather than increase employment opportunities for women workers. He also asserted that the rules would infringe upon male supervisors' freedom of expression and create antagonism toward female employees.

The hearings featured testimony by anti-feminist activists like Phyllis Schlafly (1924–2016), who embraced traditional women's roles as wives, mothers, and homemakers. Schlafly rejected the idea that sexual harassment was a form of sex discrimination and claimed that women could avoid it by carrying themselves in a modest and virtuous manner. "When a woman walks across the room, she speaks with a universal body language that most men intuitively understand," she declared. "Men hardly ever ask sexual favors of women from whom the certain answer is no" (Rich 1981). Norton, who had stepped down when Reagan took office, testified in defense of the EEOC rules. She argued that women workers were entitled to legal protection from the degradation of sexual harassment. Despite the controversy, the EEOC voted to approve the guidelines. Most government agencies and private employers soon adopted them, and they proved influential in determining the direction of future legislation and court rulings on sexual harassment.

In 1982, Reagan appointed Clarence Thomas (1948–) to head the EEOC. During his eight-year tenure at the agency, Thomas concentrated on streamlining operations and increasing efficiency, which included making budget cuts and staffing reductions. Critics contended that he also curtailed the agency's enforcement of civil rights protections for workers, especially in the area of sexual harassment. When President George H. W. Bush nominated Thomas for a seat on the U.S. Supreme Court in 1991, allegations that he had sexually harassed a female EEOC employee, Anita Hill (1956–), nearly derailed his confirmation.

Further Reading

Barnes v. Costle, 561 F. 2d 983. https://openjurist.org/561/f2d/983/barnes-v-m-costle

Corne v. Bausch and Lomb, 390 F. Supp. 161. https://law.justia.com/cases/federal/district-courts/FSupp/390/161/1966370/

Crockett, Emily. 2016. "The History of Sexual Harassment Explains Why Many Women Wait So Long to Come Forward." *Vox*, July 14. https://www.vox.com/2016/7/14/12178412/roger-ailes-sexual-harassment-history-women-wait

Crouch, Margaret A. 2001. *Thinking about Sexual Harassment: A Guide for the Perplexed.* New York: Oxford University Press.

Equal Employment Opportunity Commission. 1990. "Policy Guidance on Current Issues of Sexual Harassment." Notice N-915-050. https://www.eeoc.gov/policy/docs/currentissues.html

MacKinnon, Catharine A. 1979. *Sexual Harassment of Working Women.* New Haven, CT: Yale University Press.

Rich, Spencer. 1981. "Sexual Harassment on the Job No Problem for Virtuous Women." *Washington Post*, April 22. https://www.washingtonpost.com/archive/politics/1981/04/22/schlafly-sex-harassment-on-job-no-problem-for-virtuous-women/d3defdf6-19fa-4db2-b307-4c40ff592455/?utm_term=.e45ab4e51ca4

The U.S. Supreme Court Recognizes Sexual Harassment (1986)

The guidelines issued by the Equal Opportunity Employment Commission (EEOC) in 1980 recognized two forms of sexual harassment in the workplace: quid pro quo, in which sexual compliance is required in exchange for employment opportunity, and hostile work environment, in which a persistent pattern of abusive behavior affects the conditions of employment. The EEOC defined both types of sexual harassment as sex discrimination prohibited under Title VII of the Civil Rights Act of 1964.

A series of federal court decisions in the late 1970s established employer liability for quid pro quo sexual harassment that caused economic injury to an employee. Economic injury included such tangible harm as losing a job, being denied a promotion or wage increase, or having employment benefits withheld. If a supervisor threatened to fire a subordinate for rejecting sexual advances, for instance, the subordinate could sue both the supervisor and the employer for unlawful sex discrimination. In the early years of sexual harassment litigation, however, the courts were less clear about whether employers could be held liable for a hostile work environment that caused noneconomic injury, such as psychological harm, to an employee.

When the first sexual harassment case reached the U.S. Supreme Court in 1986, feminists and legal observers watched with great anticipation. The nation's highest court has the final word in American jurisprudence, so its interpretation of Title VII's protections against sex discrimination in employment had the potential to impact the lives of millions of working women. In addition, the case it agreed to hear, *Meritor Savings Bank v. Vinson*, 477 U.S. 57, concerned the relatively unsettled question of whether employers were liable for sexual harassment that created a hostile work environment.

The Case of Mechelle Vinson

Mechelle Vinson became a bank teller trainee at Capital City Federal Savings and Loan Association in Washington, D.C., in 1974, when she was 19 years old. Sidney L. Taylor, the branch manager and assistant vice president, hired her and became her supervisor. According to Vinson, Taylor sexually harassed her from 1975 to 1977. She claimed that Taylor touched her inappropriately, exposed himself to her, demanded sexual favors, and forcibly raped her on several occasions. Vinson estimated that she had sexual intercourse with Taylor 40–50 times during the course of her employment. She described his sexual advances as unwelcome and said she felt coerced into participating by the fear of losing her job.

In 1978, Vinson informed her employer, by then known as Meritor Savings Bank, that she was taking indefinite sick leave. A short time later, Taylor fired her for excessive time off work. Vinson then filed a civil lawsuit against both Taylor and Meritor, charging that she had been subjected to severe and pervasive sexual harassment as a condition of her employment, which had created a hostile work environment in violation of Title VII. Vinson asked the district court to grant an injunction prohibiting Taylor's actions as well as compensatory and punitive damages.

During the district court hearing, Taylor denied having a sexual relationship with Vinson and claimed that her allegations of sexual harassment arose from a business dispute. Likewise, Meritor Savings Bank rejected Vinson's allegation of a hostile work environment. Meritor's lawyers insisted the employer could not be held liable for Taylor's conduct because Vinson had never notified company management that Taylor had violated its nondiscrimination policies. They also pointed out that Vinson had neither taken advantage of the bank's grievance process nor filed charges with the EEOC. For her part, Vinson said fear of retaliation by Taylor prevented her from filing a grievance. Her attorneys also argued that Taylor perpetrated the sexual harassment as an agent of the bank—using the authority delegated to him as a supervisor—which made the employer responsible for his actions.

The bank's attorneys called witnesses who testified that Vinson had dressed provocatively and discussed sexual fantasies with other employees at work. They argued that Vinson's participation in sexual activity with Taylor had been voluntary, rather than conditional to her employment. The court refused to hear testimony from other female bank employees who claimed that Taylor had fondled them, which Vinson's lawyers said established a pattern of harassment that contributed to the hostile work environment. The district court ruled in favor of Taylor and the bank, asserting that Vinson had failed to prove her case for sex discrimination.

Vinson appealed the ruling to the U.S. Court of Appeals for the District of Columbia. In 1985, the appeals court reversed the earlier ruling and issued a decision in favor of Vinson. The judges found that the lower court had erred by excluding testimony from other female bank employees that established a pattern of sexual harassment. They also rejected the lower court's finding that Vinson could not claim sexual harassment if her participation had been voluntary. According to the appeals court, the key question was whether Vinson considered Taylor's sexual advances unwelcome. In that case, she was still entitled to legal redress—even if she had submitted voluntarily in order to keep her job—because she had felt compelled to tolerate Taylor's behavior as a condition of her employment. The judges also faulted the lower court for failing to evaluate Vinson's claim that Taylor's conduct created a hostile work environment. Finally, they ruled that Meritor was liable for sexual harassment by supervisory personnel even if the employer had not been notified about it.

The Supreme Court Weighs In

In order to resolve these conflicting rulings, the Supreme Court heard oral arguments in the case of *Meritor Savings Bank v. Vinson* on March 26, 1986. Three months later, on June 19, the justices ruled 9–0 in favor of Vinson. The opinion of the court, written by Justice William H. Rehnquist (1924–2005), said that Congress had intended for Title VII to "strike at the entire spectrum of disparate treatment of men and women in employment." Under this broad interpretation of federal civil rights law, the court recognized sexual harassment as an actionable offense. "When a supervisor sexually harasses a subordinate because of the subordinate's sex, that supervisor 'discriminates' on the basis of sex," Rehnquist wrote.

In addition, the court ruled that employees did not have to suffer tangible, economic injury from quid pro quo sexual harassment to be entitled to legal redress. Instead, the justices found that sex discrimination also occurred when an employee suffered noneconomic injury to their psychological well-being from a hostile work environment. Quoting from a 1982 appeals court decision, *Henson v. Dundee*, Rehnquist noted that "sexual harassment which creates a hostile or offensive environment for members of one sex is every bit the arbitrary barrier to sexual equality at the workplace that racial harassment is to racial equality. Surely, a requirement that a man or woman run a gauntlet of sexual abuse in return for the privilege of being allowed to work and make a living can be as demeaning and disconcerting as the harshest of racial epithets." Rehnquist went on to note that an occasional, passing offensive remark or sexual advance would not meet the definition of a hostile working environment. Rather, the court ruled that the sexual harassment must be severe or pervasive enough to alter the conditions of employment in order to violate Title VII.

The Supreme Court also rejected the claim that Vinson's participation in sexual activity with her boss was voluntary and thus precluded a legal claim of sexual harassment. It recognized that the hierarchical nature of the employment relationship gave a supervisor coercive power over a subordinate, which meant that a subordinate might voluntarily submit to sexual advances that were nevertheless unwelcome. "The correct inquiry is whether respondent by her conduct indicated that the alleged sexual advances were unwelcome, not whether her actual participation in sexual intercourse was voluntary," Rehnquist wrote. The justices did rule, however, that the testimony about Vinson's apparel and behavior in the workplace was allowable because it helped determine whether she had found Taylor's sexual advances unwelcome.

To the disappointment of women's rights activists, the Supreme Court declined to issue a definitive ruling on the extent of employer liability for sexual harassment in the workplace. Instead, Rehnquist noted that employer liability depended on the circumstances of the case. In an assessment of the decision for the *Columbia Law Review*, one legal scholar asserted that "the issue courts have found most troubling in cases of environmental sex harassment by supervisors" had been left unresolved (Anderson 1987). Other analysts took a more optimistic view of the decision, however, and expressed hope that it would encourage employers to put policies in place to eliminate sexual harassment in order to comply with Title VII and avoid legal liability (Bartels 1987).

Further Reading

Anderson, Katherine S. 1987. "Employer Liability under Title VII for Sexual Harassment after *Meritor Savings Bank v. Vinson*." *Columbia Law Review* 87(6): 1258–1279.

Bartels, Victoria T. 1987. "*Meritor Savings Bank v. Vinson*: The Supreme Court's Recognition of the Hostile Environment in Sexual Harassment Claims." *Akron Law Review* 20(3): 575–589. https://www.uakron.edu/dotAsset/e4ef57bd-5bd9-4b86-8bf5-0bcab16ddc43.pdf

Cochran, Augustus B. 2004. *Sexual Harassment and the Law: The Mechelle Vinson Case*. Lawrence: University Press of Kansas.

Meritor Savings Bank v. Vinson, 477 U.S. 57. https://supreme.justia.com/cases/federal/us/477/57/case.html

Taylor, Stuart, Jr. 1986. "Sex Harassment on Job Is Illegal." *New York Times*, June 20. https://www.nytimes.com/1986/06/20/us/sex-harassment-on-job-is-illegal.html

The Clarence Thomas–Anita Hill Hearings (1991)

Five years after the U.S. Supreme Court issued its first decision on sexual harassment in *Meritor Savings Bank v. Vinson*, the Senate confirmation hearings for Supreme Court nominee Clarence Thomas (1948–) turned into a public inquisition over allegations that he had sexually harassed a former employee, Anita Hill (1956–). The controversial hearings received intensive, round-the-clock media coverage, which brought the issue of sexual harassment out of the shadows and into the spotlight. As the first notable case of a high-profile public figure being accused of sexual harassment, the Thomas–Hill hearings marked a watershed moment in raising national awareness of unfair treatment of women in the workplace and in the American political system.

Controversy Surrounds Confirmation Hearings

In October 1991, Justice Thurgood Marshall (1908–1993) announced his retirement after 24 years of service on the U.S. Supreme Court. Prior to becoming the first African American Supreme Court justice in 1967, Marshall was a renowned civil rights lawyer whose arguments in *Brown v. Board of Education* led to the landmark 1954 ruling that outlawed racial segregation in public schools. To fill the vacancy, Republican President George H. W. Bush (1924–) nominated Clarence Thomas, a 43-year-old African American attorney and federal administrator. Thomas was known for his conservative political views, which made him the ideological opposite of Marshall. In his eight-year tenure as head of the Equal Employment Opportunity Commission (EEOC), for instance, Thomas opposed the use of affirmative action policies to remedy past discrimination against women, racial minorities, and other historically marginalized groups.

During the first round of Thomas's confirmation hearings before the Senate Judiciary Committee, some of the most contentious questions concerned his views on abortion. Thomas insisted that he had not formed a strong opinion on the matter and would decide any cases on the basis of constitutional law. Some committee members also raised concerns about his lack of judicial experience, since Thomas had served as a federal judge for less than two years prior to his nomination. Despite vocal opposition from women's rights and civil rights groups, it initially appeared as if

Thomas would win confirmation easily. Shortly before the committee concluded its work, however, a confidential Federal Bureau of Investigation background report about Thomas was leaked to the press. This report included detailed allegations made by Anita Hill, a 35-year-old African American law professor, that the nominee had sexually harassed her a decade earlier. When news of the accusations became public, the Judiciary Committee launched a new round of hearings and invited Hill to testify.

Hill appeared before the committee—comprising 14 senators, all of whom were white males—on October 11, 1991. In her testimony, she noted that she had worked as an assistant to Thomas at the U.S. Department of Education and then at the EEOC from 1981 to 1983. During that time, Hill claimed that Thomas subjected her to a pattern of inappropriate remarks and offensive conduct in the workplace. She accused Thomas of repeatedly asking her out on dates, commenting on her clothing or appearance, discussing sexually explicit topics, and bragging about his sexual prowess. Hill testified that Thomas "spoke about acts that he had seen in pornographic films involving such matters as women having sex with animals and films showing group sex or rape scenes. He talked about pornographic materials depicting individuals with large penises or large breasts involved in various sex acts." Hill also alleged that Thomas had once approached her desk and asked, "Who has put pubic hair on my Coke?" (Miller 1994, 23).

After reading her prepared statement, Hill answered questions from members of the Judiciary Committee. As millions of Americans watched on television, the senators took turns delving into various aspects of Hill's testimony. The question-and-answer session quickly assumed a partisan tenor. Republican committee members, in the interest of protecting Bush's conservative nominee, attacked Hill's credibility, questioned her motivations for coming forward, and insisted that she had misrepresented or misinterpreted Thomas's behavior. Democratic committee members, led by Chairman Joseph Biden (1942–), seemed reluctant to defend Hill or intervene in the Republicans' aggressive cross-examination. Biden also came under criticism from feminists for failing to call witnesses who were available to corroborate Hill's testimony—either friends whom she had told about Thomas's behavior or coworkers who had also experienced it. "The Democrats sought to be fair to Thomas; the Republicans fought to convict Hill," wrote former State Department employee Wendy R. Sherman. "The Republicans succeeded" (Sherman 2017).

For his part, Thomas adamantly rejected Hill's accusations. "I deny each and every single allegation against me today that suggested in any way that I had conversations of a sexual nature or about pornographic material with

Anita Hill, that I ever attempted to date her, that I ever had any personal sexual interest in her, or that I in any way ever harassed her," he declared. Thomas angrily condemned the Judiciary Committee for allowing Hill to testify, which he characterized as a blatantly racist attempt to discredit and disqualify him. "From my standpoint, as a black American, as far as I'm concerned, it is a high-tech lynching for uppity blacks who in any way deign to think for themselves, to do for themselves, to have different ideas. And it is a message that unless you kowtow to an old order, this is what will happen to you. You will be lynched, destroyed, caricatured by a committee of the U.S. Senate, rather than hung from a tree" (Miller 1994, 118).

Lasting Impact of the Hearings

Public opinion about the dramatic hearings also tended to be divided along partisan lines. Most Republicans, and especially men, doubted Hill's allegations and insisted that a federal judge on the cusp of Supreme Court confirmation would never commit perjury. Most Democrats, and especially women, believed Hill's allegations and argued that no one would willingly endure such public scrutiny over fabricated charges of sexual harassment. In the end, the Senate voted 52–48—the closest margin in a century—to confirm Thomas to a lifetime appointment on the Supreme Court.

Feminists and others who opposed Thomas's nomination were outraged that the Judiciary Committee did not investigate Hill's allegations more fully. They viewed Thomas's confirmation as a political defeat and worried that his presence on the court would set back the cause of women's rights. By increasing public awareness of sexual harassment in the workplace, however, the controversial hearings helped many women overcome feelings of shame and gather the courage to speak out against it. As a result, the number of sexual harassment claims filed with the EEOC rose dramatically in the wake of Hill's testimony—from 6,883 in 1991 to 15,618 in 1998 (EEOC 2010). Anger and disgust over the dismissive treatment of Hill by the all-male Judiciary Committee also convinced a record number of women to run for public office in 1992. Five female candidates were elected to the U.S. Senate that year, and 24 more joined the U.S. House of Representatives.

Several of the key figures involved in the Thomas–Hill controversy have remained prominent in the nearly three decades since then. Biden left the Senate in 2009 to serve as vice president under President Barack Obama (1961–). As Biden contemplated a presidential run in 2020, however, his handling of Thomas's confirmation hearings came under renewed criticism, and some analysts speculated that it could become a political liability for him in a climate of low tolerance for sexual harassment. Thomas still sat on the Supreme Court as of 2018, where he developed a reputation as its most conservative justice. As allegations of sexual harassment derailed the careers of other prominent political figures, a growing number of critics called for a renewed investigation into the allegations against him, which they viewed as potential grounds for impeachment.

Meanwhile, Hill retreated from the public eye and built a successful career as a law professor. As the #MeToo movement focused new attention on sexual harassment, Hill emerged as a spokesperson for victims. In 2017, she accepted a position as chair of the Commission on Sexual Harassment and Advancing Equality in the Workplace, an organization dedicated to addressing discriminatory and abusive practices in the entertainment industry. "The energy and even anger of this moment says we are ready to end sexual harassment," she declared. "We are ready to take on the deniers and enablers and ready to share our truth" (Flores 2017).

Further Reading

Equal Opportunity Employment Commission (EEOC). 2010. "Enforcement Guidance: Vicarious Employer Liability for Unlawful Harassment by Supervisors." https://www.eeoc.gov/policy/docs/harassment.pdf

Flores, Nancy. 2017. "Anita Hill in Austin: We Are Ready to End Sexual Harassment." *Austin American-Statesman*, November 2. https://www.mystatesman.com/news/local/anita-hill-are-ready-end-sexual-harassment/MdjX7wUHpCzNrNzhkRFBHN/

Graham, David A. 2017. "The Clarence Thomas Exception." *Atlantic*, December 20. https://www.theatlantic.com/politics/archive/2017/12/clarence-thomas-anita-hill-me-too/548624/

Hill, Anita F. 1997. *Speaking Truth to Power*. New York: Doubleday.

Mayer, Jane, and Jill Abramson. 1994. *Strange Justice: The Selling of Clarence Thomas*. Boston: Houghton Mifflin.

Miller, Anita, ed. 1994. *The Complete Transcripts of the Clarence Thomas–Anita Hill Hearings*. Chicago: Academy Chicago Publishers.

Sherman, Wendy. 2017. "I Helped Anita Hill Testify against Clarence Thomas. That Hearing Gave Lie to Our Current Reality." *Time*, November 9. http://time.com/5018066/anita-hill-sexual-assault-hearing-harvey-weinstein/

Thomas, Clarence. 2007. *My Grandfather's Son: A Memoir*. New York: Harper.

The Tailhook Convention Scandal (1991)

The Thirty-Fifth Annual Tailhook Association Symposium took place in September 1991, just a few weeks before the controversial Clarence

Thomas–Anita Hill hearings launched a national conversation about sexual harassment. The Tailhook Association is a fraternal organization for U.S. military personnel involved in sea-based aviation, including active duty, reserve, and retired service members from the Navy, Marines, and Coast Guard. The organization's name comes from the apparatus beneath a plane that is used to catch an arresting cable while landing on the deck of an aircraft carrier. Members of the Tailhook Association gathered for an annual convention from the time of the group's founding in 1956. During these events, the aviators attended presentations, shared information, bestowed awards and scholarships, and socialized.

Around 4,000 military personnel and 1,000 defense contractors attended the 1991 Tailhook Convention at the Las Vegas Hilton in Nevada. The professional presentations focused on military aviation during Operation Desert Storm (1990–1991), the successful, six-month-long effort by a U.S.-led military coalition to liberate Kuwait from Iraqi occupation. American aviators who had contributed to the coalition victory in the Persian Gulf were greeted as returning heroes, and the festivities assumed a celebratory air. Even before 1991, many Tailhook members viewed the annual symposium as an opportunity to cut loose and enjoy time off from rigid military rules and discipline. Squadrons from different branches of service always hosted parties in hospitality suites on the third floor of the hotel and competed to attract the biggest crowds.

Some attendees felt that the atmosphere of the 1991 convention was tinged with an element of animosity toward women that had not been as prominent a feature of previous events. More than 40,000 American women served in the Persian Gulf War, making it the largest deployment of military women in U.S. history. Although federal law prohibited women from serving in direct combat roles at that time, opportunities for female service members expanded greatly during the war. Some male service members resented the changes, which they felt would detract from traditional "warrior culture" of the military, and worried about increased competition for choice assignments. A female Navy commander remembered encountering such attitudes among male aviators. "This was the woman that was making you, you know, change your ways," she noted. "This was the woman that was threatening your livelihood. This was the woman that wanted to take your spot in that combat aircraft" (Frontline 1996). Some male Tailhook attendees wore T-shirts adorned with such slogans as "Women Are Property" or "He-Man Woman-Haters Club," making it clear that they did not welcome the presence of women in the military ranks.

Sexual Assaults Mar the Convention

In the evenings, the 1991 Tailhook Convention turned into a raucous, hard-partying affair, full of drunkenness and lewd behavior. The third-floor hospitality suites, the adjacent pool area, and the hallways connecting them became the center of the late-night action for rowdy aviators. Several of the parties hired strippers or prostitutes to cater to their guests. Some drunken attendees amused themselves by mooning each other, exposing their genitals, or streaking across the outdoor patio. Couples participated in "chicken fights" in the pool, where women being carried on men's shoulders tried to yank off each other's bikini tops. Some women allowed men to shave their legs or to "zap" them by placing squadron-logo stickers on their bodies. By spilling drinks, dropping cigarettes, urinating, vomiting, breaking windows, and engaging in acts of vandalism, the revelers caused an estimated $23,000 in property damage (Gross 1993).

Although immature, disrespectful, and inappropriate behavior was commonplace at the convention, most attendees viewed it as harmless, drunken fun among consenting adults. In many cases, however, attendees' behavior crossed the line into sexual misconduct, harassment, or assault. A series of incidents occurred in the third-floor hallway outside the hospitality suites, known as the Gantlet (or Gauntlet), which was typically packed with hundreds of drunken aviators in the evenings. Whenever a woman approached the crowded hallway, a scout would yell "clear deck" if she was attractive and unaccompanied, or "wave off" if she was unattractive or with an officer. If a woman tried to pass through the crowd, the men would go crazy—whistling, shouting, fondling, pinching, groping, grabbing, and tearing off her clothing. Many women endured physical or sexual assaults that left them bruised and bloody, and some had to be rescued by hotel security guards. During the three nights of the convention, the Gantlet victimized at least 83 women and 7 men (Frontline 1996).

The president of the Tailhook Association, Captain Frederic G. Ludwig, expressed dismay at the extent of the damage and debauchery that occurred during the 1991 convention. "I have five separate reports of young ladies, several of whom had nothing to do with Tailhook, who were verbally abused, had drinks thrown at them, were physically abused and were sexually molested," he wrote in a letter to members dated October 11, 1991. "I don't have to tell you that this type of behavior has put a very serious blemish on what was otherwise a successful symposium. It has further given a black eye to the Tailhook Association and all Naval Aviation. Our ability to conduct future Tailhooks has been put at great risk due to the rampant unprofessionalism of a few. Tailhook cannot and will not condone the blatant and total disregard of individual rights and public/private property!" (Frontline 1996).

On October 29, then secretary of the Navy H. Lawrence Garrett III (1939–) responded to Ludwig's letter by withdrawing official U.S. Navy support from the Tailhook Association. "No man who holds a commission in this Navy will ever subject a woman to the kind of abuse in evidence at Tailhook '91 with impunity," he wrote in a letter to members. "And no organization which makes possible this behavior is in any way worthy of a naval leadership or advisory role" (Frontline 1996). Garrett also ordered the Naval Investigative Service, under the leadership of Rear Admiral Duvall M. Williams Jr., to launch an investigation into the allegations of misconduct by military personnel at the convention.

After interviewing people who attended the symposium, the Naval Investigative Service issued a report in April 1992. Although it acknowledged that some low-ranking enlisted personnel had behaved inappropriately, it denied that high-ranking officers bore any responsibility for their actions. Assistant Secretary of the Navy for Manpower and Reserve Affairs Barbara S. Pope (1951–) objected to the report's conclusions. She argued that Williams and others had intentionally impeded the investigation in order to protect senior officers and avoid negative publicity. She claimed that Williams had made derogatory statements about women in her presence, such as comparing female Navy pilots to "topless dancers and hookers" (Schmitt 1992), and she questioned his ability to conduct an objective investigation. Pope threatened to resign unless Garrett approved a new, more extensive inquiry into the allegations surrounding the Tailhook convention.

Paula Coughlin Goes Public

In the meantime, women who were sexually assaulted in the Gantlet grew increasingly frustrated by the military's disinterested response to their allegations. Lieutenant Paula A. Coughlin (1962–), a Navy helicopter pilot and admiral's aide, had described her traumatic experience to her supervisor the next morning. "I got attacked by a bunch of men that tried to pull my clothes off," she reported. "I fell down to the floor and tried to get out of the hallway, and they wouldn't let me out. They were trying to pull my underwear off from between my legs…. If I didn't make it off the floor, I was sure I was going to be gang raped" (Noble 1994). Her supervisor dismissed her complaint, saying that she should have expected as much when she entered a hallway full of drunken aviators. When Coughlin told other Navy officers about her experience, they criticized her for making a big deal out of a good-natured Tailhook tradition, questioned her judgment for consuming alcohol and wearing a short skirt, advised her to seek counseling, or warned her that bringing charges against her attackers would destroy her career.

Despite facing intense pressure to drop the matter, Coughlin continued to pursue it. She felt personally betrayed by her fellow aviators and recognized that permissive attitudes toward sexual misconduct would make it impossible for women to succeed in the military. "I had worked my a** off trying to be one of the guys," she declared, "to be the best naval officer I can and prove women can do whatever the job calls for" (Boo 1992). Coughlin was outraged by the conclusions presented in the Naval Investigative Service report, which made it seem as if the Navy was unwilling to take meaningful action to prevent the denigration of women. In June 1992, Coughlin decided to go public. She took her story to the news media, and national coverage of her allegations created a major scandal that rocked the U.S. military.

The Inspector General of the Department of Defense launched a second investigation into the Tailhook convention. In September 1992, the Pentagon released a 2,000-page report that sharply criticized the Navy's earlier inquiry. Investigators spoke with dozens of witnesses and survivors who corroborated Coughlin's account of her experiences in the Gantlet. "Many eyewitness accounts described women who had articles of clothing ripped or removed as they went through the gantlet," the report noted. "One particularly disturbing incident involved an intoxicated college freshman who was stripped from the waist down as she was passed overhead through the gantlet and then left on the hallway floor.... A female civilian victim told us that, as she walked up the hallway, at least seven men attacked her. They pulled down her 'tube top' and grabbed at her exposed breasts while she attempted to cover herself with her arms" (Kempster 1993).

Armed with the Inspector General's report, the Pentagon imposed disciplinary action that harmed or ended the careers of 14 admirals and 300 aviators. Defense officials also instituted a number of policy changes designed to eliminate hostility toward women in military culture and ensure that female service members received equal opportunities for career advancement. These policy shifts eventually lifted the ban on women serving in combat positions. Supporters hoped that improving conditions for women in the military would lead to greater equality in other aspects of American life.

Such changes generated anger and resentment among some government officials and members of the military, however. Critics claimed that allowing women in combat would cause distractions, harm morale, destroy cohesion in military units, and reduce battle readiness. They viewed the Tailhook investigations as a "witch hunt" based on inaccurate information and unsubstantiated allegations. They claimed that overblown media coverage of the "scandal" destroyed the careers and reputations of dozens of valuable officers. Critics noted that some service members were denied promotions merely for having attended Tailhook in 1991, even if they had never been accused of any wrongdoing, and pointed out that one decorated officer had been forced to retire even though he had only appeared at the convention to receive an award.

Coughlin retired from the Navy in 1994 due to retaliation she faced as a whistleblower. She settled in Florida, became a yoga instructor, and withdrew from the public eye for more than a decade. In 2012, she appeared in *The Invisible War*, a documentary about rape in the U.S. military that was nominated for an Academy Award. Coughlin then joined the board of directors of Protect Our Defenders, a nonprofit group that advocates for members of the military who have experienced sexual assault. Unwelcome sexual contact and sexual violence remain serious problems in the U.S. armed forces. The Pentagon reported that 20,000 service members were raped or sexually assaulted in 2014. Only 13 percent of reported cases resulted in a court-martial, however, and only 4 percent ended in convictions. In addition, 62 percent of military women who reported sexual assault or rape ended up being targeted for retaliation (Coughlin 2017).

Further Reading

Boo, Katherine. 1992. "Universal Soldier: What Paula Coughlin Can Teach American Women." *Washington Monthly*, September. https://www.pbs.org/wgbh/pages/frontline/shows/navy/tailhook/debate.html#us

Coughlin, Paula. 2017. "Marine Nude Photos a Leadership Disaster: Tailhook Whistleblower." *USA Today*, March 9. https://www.usatoday.com/story/opinion/2017/03/09/military-failing-women-decades-paula-coughlin-column/98909892/

Frontline. 1996. "The Navy Blues: The Clash of Values and Politics in the Post-Tailhook Navy." PBS. https://www.pbs.org/wgbh/pages/frontline/shows/navy/tailhook/rat.html

Gross, Jane. 1993. "Tailhook Aviators Trying to Regroup." *New York Times*, October 8. https://www.nytimes.com/1993/10/08/us/tailhook-aviators-trying-to-regroup.html

Kempster, Norman. 1993. "What Really Happened at Tailhook Convention." *Los Angeles Times*, April 24. http://articles.latimes.com/1993-04-24/news/mn-26672_1_tailhook-convention

Noble, Kenneth B. 1994. "Tailhook Whistle-Blower Recalls Attack." *New York Times*, October 4. https://www.nytimes.com/1994/10/04/us/tailhook-whistle-blower-recalls-attack.html

Schmitt, Eric. 1992. "Senior Navy Officers Suppressed Sex Investigation, Pentagon Says." *New York Times*, September 25. https://www.nytimes.com/1992/09/25/us/senior-navy-officers-suppressed-sex-investigation-pentagon-says.html

Employers Gain the *Faragher–Ellerth* Defense (1998)

In its 1986 ruling in *Meritor Savings Bank v. Vinson*, the U.S. Supreme Court recognized sexual harassment in the workplace as an actionable offense under Title VII of the Civil Rights Act of 1964. It found that unlawful sex discrimination could occur when an employee suffered tangible, economic injury from quid pro quo sexual harassment, as well as when an employee suffered noneconomic injury to his or her psychological well-being from a hostile work environment. The court stopped short, however, of providing definitive guidance on the extent of employer liability for sexual harassment. For the next dozen years, legal experts wrangled over the question of when employers could be held responsible for sexual harassment perpetrated by supervisors, while employers debated about what steps they could take to protect themselves from liability.

On June 26, 1998, the Supreme Court issued a pair of rulings that provided more clarity on the issue of employer liability for sexual harassment. Taken together, the court's decisions in the companion cases of *Faragher v. City of Boca Raton*, 524 U.S. 775, and *Burlington Industries, Inc. v. Ellerth*, 524 U.S. 742, created a two-pronged, affirmative defense for employers seeking to avoid liability and damages for alleged sexual harassment that created a hostile work environment. The *Faragher–Ellerth* defense did not apply in cases where quid pro quo sexual harassment by a supervisor resulted in a tangible, adverse employment outcome for the employee, such as being fired, demoted, or reassigned to a less desirable job. In these cases, the employer maintained strict or automatic liability. In the absence of a tangible economic injury, however, an employer could apply the *Faragher–Ellerth* defense by proving the following two conditions:

1. The employer took reasonable care to prevent sexual harassment from occurring in the workplace, and took prompt, appropriate action to correct any such behavior that did occur.
2. The employee unreasonably failed to take advantage of readily accessible preventive or corrective measures offered by the employer to avoid being harmed by sexual harassment in the workplace.

For an employer, "reasonable care" to prevent sexual harassment might include establishing, distributing, and enforcing clear anti-harassment policies; providing mandatory training programs to help supervisors understand, recognize, and avoid sexual harassment; promptly investigating sexual harassment complaints and taking appropriate disciplinary action when warranted; and protecting employees who file sexual harassment complaints from retaliation. For an employee, "unreasonably" failing to avoid harm might encompass not informing a human resources or union representative of the harassment, not following a formal grievance procedure or using a complaint hotline, or otherwise not seeking relief through means offered by the employer. To be eligible to use the *Faragher–Ellerth* defense against claims of a hostile work environment, an employer must prove by a "preponderance of evidence" that both conditions existed.

The Namesake Cases

The *Faragher–Ellerth* defense gets its name from the two plaintiffs who received favorable judgments from the Supreme Court in 1998. Beth Ann Faragher worked part time as a lifeguard for the City of Boca Raton, Florida, from 1985 to 1990. Throughout the course of her employment, she asserted that her two male supervisors created a hostile work environment by speaking about women in offensive terms, making vulgar references to sexual acts and body parts, threatening to withhold promotions or assign undesirable job duties if she refused to date them, and subjecting her to constant, unwanted, inappropriate touching. Other female lifeguards corroborated Faragher's accounts and reported having experienced the same sort of behavior by the two men.

In 1992, Faragher filed a lawsuit against her former supervisors and the City of Boca Raton, claiming that she had endured a pervasive pattern of abusive conduct that affected the conditions of her employment and created a hostile work environment. The district court ruled in favor of Faragher, concluding that she had experienced discriminatory sexual harassment in violation of Title VII. The court found Boca Raton liable because the supervisors were acting as agents of the city when the harassment occurred. The Eleventh Circuit Court of Appeals reversed the judgment against Boca Raton, however, arguing that city officials were not liable because they had no knowledge of the harassment.

When *Faragher v. Boca Raton* reached the Supreme Court in 1998, the justices overturned the appeals court decision and ruled in favor of Faragher. The 7–2 decision, penned by Justice David Souter (1939–), stated that an employer could be subject to vicarious liability for sexual harassment by a supervisor that created a hostile work environment, even if the employee did not suffer any tangible economic injury. The ruling also set forth a clear, objective standard for determining employer liability in such cases, which featured the two-pronged, affirmative defense for employers. The court found that the actions taken by Boca Raton officials did not meet the conditions for this defense, so it held the city liable for discriminatory behavior by Faragher's supervisors.

Kimberly Ellerth, the plaintiff in the second case, worked as a salesperson for Burlington Industries in Chicago from 1993 to 1994. She claimed that she had been forced to quit her job after 15 months because a male supervisor subjected her to offensive remarks, lewd gestures, and unwanted sexual advances. Ellerth also alleged that the supervisor threatened to withhold promotions and other job benefits unless she granted him sexual favors. Ellerth never informed company management about the situation, even though she was aware that Burlington Industries had a policy against sexual harassment.

The district court dismissed Ellerth's claim because she had not suffered any adverse job consequences by rejecting her supervisor's advances. The Seventh Circuit Court of Appeals reversed the lower court's decision and ruled—in eight separate opinions—in favor of Ellerth. Finally, the Supreme Court weighed in, issuing a 7–2 decision upholding the appeals court ruling. The majority opinion in *Burlington Industries v. Ellerth*, written by Justice Anthony Kennedy (1936–), reiterated the principles established in the companion case for determining employer liability in cases where sexual harassment did not cause tangible economic harm to the employee. While the court found that Ellerth's supervisor created a hostile work environment, it also offered Burlington Industries an opportunity to raise an affirmative defense against liability and damages.

Interpretations and Applications

The Supreme Court's *Faragher–Ellerth* decisions aroused controversy. Some legal scholars denounced the rulings, claiming that they created an avenue for employers to escape liability for sexual harassment and erected a barrier to justice for employees who were victimized by sexual harassment. Other commentators praised the decisions, arguing that they provided a fair, objective method for courts to use in evaluating sexual harassment claims and determining employer liability. Many employers used the guidelines set forth by the Supreme Court to develop and implement strong new policies and training programs aimed at preventing sexual harassment. Many companies also adopted new processes and procedures to encourage employees to come forward with sexual harassment complaints.

In the two decades since the *Faragher–Ellerth* rulings, many state and local jurisdictions have adopted antidiscrimination laws modeled upon Title VII. In a few cases, where these laws have provided for strict employer liability in cases of sexual harassment by supervisors, courts have disallowed use of the *Faragher–Ellerth* defense. In 2009, for instance, a federal court in New York rejected the *Faragher–Ellerth* defense in *Zakrzewska v. The New School*, ruling that it was incompatible with the New York City Human Rights Law. That same year, the Illinois Supreme Court ruled that the Illinois Human Rights Act precluded an employer from using the *Faragher–Ellerth* defense in *Sangamon County Sheriff's Department v. The Illinois Department of Human Rights*. Some legal scholars asserted that such interpretations signaled a shift in sexual harassment law favoring employee rights, while others contended that the variation between federal, state, and local laws only made the legal landscape more confusing.

Further Reading

Burlington Industries, Inc. v. Ellerth, 524 U.S. 742. Justia. https://supreme.justia.com/cases/federal/us/524/742/case.html

Faragher v. City of Boca Raton, 524 U.S. 775. Justia. https://supreme.justia.com/cases/federal/us/524/775/case.html

Jacobs, Amy N. 2017. "Faragher/Ellerth to Fox News; The More Things Change, the More They Stay the Same" (whitepaper). *Employment Practice Solutions*, May 23. http://www.epspros.com/news-resources/whitepapers/2017/faragher-ellerth-to-fox-news-the-more-things-change-the-more-they-stay-the-same.html

Simmons, Jasmine. 2010. "Cities and States and Title VII … Oh My!—The Continued Viability of the Faragher–Ellerth Affirmative Defense in Light of Discrepancies among Federal, State and Local Discrimination Laws." *American Bar Association*. https://www.americanbar.org/content/dam/aba/administrative/labor_law/meetings/2010/annualconference/040.authcheckdam.pdf

Vance v. Ball State Narrows Employer Liability (2013)

In 2013, the U.S. Supreme Court issued a controversial 5–4 ruling in *Vance v. Ball State University*, 570 U.S. ___, which significantly narrowed the scope of employer liability for sexual harassment. The key question facing the court involved the definition of the term "supervisor." Title VII of the Civil Rights Act of 1964 made employers subject to vicarious liability for discriminatory conduct by supervisors. Since employers gave supervisors independent authority to act on their behalf in employment matters, the law considered supervisors to be agents of the employer and held employers responsible for their behavior. A different standard applied, however, in cases of sexual harassment by coworkers without supervisory authority. In these instances, employers faced liability only if they were negligent in taking steps to prevent or respond to discriminatory conduct in the workplace.

The Supreme Court sought to clarify the concept of employer liability for sexual harassment 15 years earlier in the companion cases of Faragher v. City of Boca Raton and Burlington Industries, Inc. v. Ellerth. These 1998 rulings established the *Faragher–Ellerth* defense, which gave employers an opportunity to avoid liability for sexual harassment by supervisors that created a hostile work environment by proving that the employer had policies and procedures in place to remedy such conduct. As various companies applied the *Faragher–Ellerth* defense, however, federal courts disagreed about what constituted a "supervisor." The Second, Fourth, and Ninth Circuit Courts of Appeals defined the term broadly to include anyone with authority to direct and oversee employees' daily work activities. The First, Seventh, and Eighth Circuit Courts, on the other hand, limited the scope of "supervisor" to include only individuals with the power to impose tangible, adverse employment consequences, such as hiring, firing, demoting, transferring, or disciplining employees.

The Supreme Court Hears the Case

The Supreme Court attempted to reconcile these differing interpretations in *Vance v. Ball State University*. The plaintiff in the case, Maetta Vance, was the only African American employee in the Banquet and Catering Department at Ball State University in Muncie, Indiana. She claimed that Saundra Davis, a white woman who worked in the department as a catering specialist, engaged in a persistent pattern of harassment and intimidation that created a racially hostile work environment in violation of Title VII. Vance accused Davis of glaring at her, blocking her entrance to an elevator, banging pots and pans near her, making derogatory remarks about her, and discriminating against her on the basis of race. Vance filed numerous complaints with the Equal Employment Opportunity Commission (EEOC) and the supervisors of her department. After investigating the situation, the supervisors required both women to attend counseling sessions on appropriate workplace behavior.

In 2006, Vance filed a lawsuit against the university, claiming that her employer was liable for Davis's discriminatory conduct. Vance contended that Davis was a supervisor because she had the power to direct and oversee Vance's day-to-day work activities. Ball State countered that Davis was not a supervisor because she lacked the authority to cause tangible economic injury or control the terms and conditions of Vance's employment. The U.S. District Court for the Southern District of Indiana ruled in favor of Ball State, concluding that Vance and Davis were coworkers. Since the university had taken appropriate corrective action by requiring both women to undergo counseling, the court said Ball State was not negligent in responding to the harassment complaints, and thus was shielded from liability. The Seventh Circuit Court of Appeals affirmed the district court's decision and adopted its narrow definition of "supervisor."

The Supreme Court granted Vance's request for appeal and heard oral arguments in *Vance v. Ball State* on November 26, 2012. Legal scholars watched closely to see which definition of "supervisor" the court would approve under Title VII and *Faragher–Ellerth*. On June 24, 2013, the court voted 5–4 to uphold the earlier decisions. The majority opinion, written by Justice Samuel Alito (1950–), asserted that the term "supervisor" only applied to individuals who were "empowered by the employer to take tangible employment actions against the victim," including "a significant change in employment status, such as hiring, firing, failing to promote, reassignment with significantly different responsibilities, or a decision causing a significant change in benefits." It did not apply to individuals who lacked such power, even if they exerted control over every other aspect of employees' day-to-day work experiences.

Justice Ruth Bader Ginsburg (1933–)—who had argued many workplace discrimination cases as a civil rights lawyer—voiced her objections in a scathing dissent. She argued that the majority decision disregarded "the conditions under which members of the workforce labor" and gutted the basic worker protections afforded by Title VII. She contended that the ruling ignored the 1980 guidelines issued by the EEOC, which had offered a broad interpretation of who qualified as a supervisor for the purposes of determining employer liability for workplace harassment. Ginsburg listed a series of real-life examples in which she said female employees would have no legal recourse against sexual harassment by bosses with apparent authority, merely because the responsibility for hiring and firing rested elsewhere. "The Court embraces a position that relieves scores of employers of responsibility for the behavior of the supervisors they employ," she wrote. "Inevitably, the Court's definition of supervisor will hinder efforts to stamp out discrimination in the workplace."

Alito responded to Ginsburg's concerns in his opinion, noting that victims of harassment by nonsupervisors could still gain legal redress by proving that their employer knew or should have known about the discriminatory conduct and failed to address it. "Assuming that a harasser is not a supervisor, a plaintiff could still prevail by showing that his or her employer was negligent in failing to prevent harassment from taking place," he wrote. "Evidence that an employer did not monitor the workplace, failed to respond to complaints, failed to provide a system for registering complaints, or effectively discouraged complaints from being filed would be relevant." Critics pointed out, however, that employers had successfully avoided liability for sexual harassment among coworkers by showing that they had anti-harassment policies and training programs in place.

Congress Reacts to the Ruling

Legal analysts described *Vance v. Ball State* as a victory for business interests, arguing that it gave employers another layer of defense against workplace discrimination claims. Workers' rights advocates asserted that the Supreme Court's decision was likely to have a chilling effect on workplace harassment claims by discouraging plaintiffs from filing Title VII lawsuits that they would face long odds of winning under the new rules. "The doors are closing on people's ability to vindicate their civil rights," said Cyrus Mehri, a prominent employment discrimination attorney. "To some extent you had a judicial repeal of Title VII" (Carmon 2013).

Some analysts claimed that *Vance v. Ball State* marked the latest in a series of Supreme Court rulings that favored the interests of employers over the rights of employees. They noted that the Chamber of Commerce, a pro-business lobbying organization, had won 70 percent of its cases decided by the conservative court led by Chief Justice John Roberts (1955–), compared to a historical average of 50 percent since World War II. "Follow this pro-business trend to its logical conclusion," warned Senator Elizabeth Warren, a Democrat from Massachusetts, "and sooner or later you'll end up with a Supreme Court that functions as a wholly owned subsidiary of the Chamber of Commerce" (Garofalo 2013).

Democrats in Congress responded to concerns expressed by workers' rights advocates by introducing the Fair Employment Protection Act (FEPA) in 2014. This legislation sought to restore the broader definition of "supervisor" that had applied under Title VII and the EEOC guidelines prior to the *Vance v. Ball State* ruling. Congress had successfully overridden *Ledbetter v. Goodyear Tire and Rubber*, a 2007 Supreme Court ruling that limited employees' ability to challenge wage discrimination, by passing the

Lilly Ledbetter Fair Pay Act of 2009. FEPA failed to generate enough support for passage, however, even when proponents re-introduced the legislation in 2017.

Further Reading

Carmon, Irin. 2013. "How Workplace Harassers Won Big." *Salon*, June 24. https://www.salon.com/2013/06/24/workplace_harassers_win_big/

Garofalo, Pat. 2013. "Score One More for the Corporations." *U.S. News and World Report*, June 24. https://www.usnews.com/opinion/blogs/pat-garofalo/2013/06/24/supreme-court-sides-with-business-in-vance-v-ball-state-harassment-case

Lee, Elizabeth. 2016. "Simplicity v. Reality in the Workplace: Balancing the Aims of *Vance v. Ball State University* and the Fair Employment Protection Act." *Hastings Law Journal* 67(6):1769. https://repository.uchastings.edu/hastings_law_journal/vol67/iss6/

Pieklo, Jessica Mason. 2013. "Justices Alito and Kennedy Mansplain Away Your Rights." *Daily Kos*, June 25. https://www.dailykos.com/stories/2013/06/25/1218723/-Justices-Alito-and-Kennedy-Mansplain-Away-Your-Rights

Vance v. Ball State University, 570 U.S. ___. Justia. https://supreme.justia.com/cases/federal/us/570/11-556/opinion3.html

The Presidential Campaign and Election of Donald Trump (2016)

The 2016 presidential election marked the first time in U.S. history that a major political party nominated a female candidate for the nation's highest office. Hillary Clinton (1947–), the Democratic candidate, had a long political career that included serving as U.S. secretary of state, U.S. senator from New York, and First Lady. The Republican candidate, Donald J. Trump (1946–), is a wealthy businessman and well-known television personality without previous political experience. The presence of a woman in the presidential race helped bring issues of gender equality and sexism to the forefront of American politics. Much of the discussion centered on Trump's behavior and rhetoric—not only toward Clinton but toward women in general—and its impact on the electorate.

Throughout the campaign, critics frequently accused Trump of making misogynistic remarks. In addition, the media unearthed incidents from his past in which he appeared to objectify or degrade women. Shortly before the November election, a recording surfaced in which Trump seemingly boasted about taking advantage of his celebrity to commit sexual assault. Several women subsequently came forward to accuse Trump of sexual misconduct. Yet such allegations did not affect Trump's standing among his most fervent supporters, some of whom attended his campaign rallies wearing T-shirts with sexist messages.

Although many female voters expressed concern about the Republican candidate's offensive comments, questionable behavior, and opposition to abortion rights, Trump still garnered 52 percent of the vote among white women, which helped lift him to the presidency. "Voters were being told constantly, 'Stare at this, care about this, make this the deal-breaker once and for all,'" explained Trump campaign manager Kellyanne Conway. "They were told that five or six times a week about different things. And yet ... they voted the way voters have always voted: on things that affect them, not just things that offend them" (Scott 2018). Other observers attributed Trump's election to public hostility toward Clinton, which they claimed was based largely on sexism (Robbins 2017).

Allegations of Sexual Misconduct during the Campaign

Trump first came under fire for making sexist comments during his primary campaign. In an August 2015 debate with other Republican hopefuls, moderator Megyn Kelly (1970–) of Fox News asked Trump about past instances when he publicly referred to women he did not like as dogs, fat pigs, or disgusting animals. A few days after this contentious exchange, Trump expressed his displeasure to a CNN interviewer by calling Kelly a "lightweight" and implying that she had questioned him so aggressively because she was menstruating. "She starts asking me all sorts of ridiculous questions, and you could see there was blood coming out of her eyes," he stated. "Blood coming out of her ... wherever" (Cohen 2017). Following a September 2015 primary debate, Trump mocked the physical appearance of the only woman in the Republican field, former Hewlett-Packard chief executive officer Carly Fiorina (1954–). "Look at that face. Would anyone vote for that?" he said to a *Rolling Stone* journalist. "Can you imagine that, the face of our next president? I mean, she's a woman, and I'm not supposed to say bad things, but really, folks, come on. Are we serious?" (Cohen 2017).

In May 2016, the *New York Times* published an article exploring Trump's treatment of women. Entitled "Crossing the Line," it was based on interviews with 50 women who encountered Trump socially or worked with him professionally over four decades. Although some of the women said they had never witnessed any sexist comments or behavior by him, many others described uncomfortable interactions that included lewd remarks, disrespectful conduct, or unwelcome sexual advances. Several of the women interviewed had been contestants in the Miss USA or Miss Teen USA beauty pageants, which Trump owned from 1996 to 2015. They claimed that Trump had entered the dressing room unannounced and ogled contestants while they dressed. Although Trump denied the charges, critics pointed out that he had described the practice to radio host Howard Stern in a 2005 interview. "I'll go backstage before a show, and everyone's getting dressed and ready and everything else," Trump declared. "And I'm allowed to go in because I'm the owner of the pageant.... You know, they're standing there with no clothes. And you see these incredible-looking women. And so I sort of get away with things like that" (Cohen 2017).

On October 3, 2016, the Associated Press released a series of interviews with former cast and crew members on *The Apprentice*, a reality-television show that Trump hosted for 14 seasons prior to his presidential run. While some people associated with the show reported having positive, professional interactions with Trump, others alleged that Trump engaged in crass, demeaning behavior toward female employees and contestants. They claimed that he rated female contestants by their appearance or the size of their breasts, asked them to dress more suggestively, and discussed which ones he wanted to have sex with. Some of the interviewees found Trump's conduct inappropriate and said it made them uncomfortable. Trump's campaign spokesperson, Hope Hicks, dismissed the charges as "outlandish, unsubstantiated, and totally false" and claimed that they had been "fabricated by publicity hungry, opportunistic, disgruntled former employees" (AP 2016).

Trump's attitude toward women came under closer scrutiny on October 7, when the *Washington Post* obtained previously unreleased video footage shot during the candidate's 2005 appearance on the entertainment show *Access Hollywood*. During a discussion with host Billy Bush, Trump appeared to brag about using the power of his wealth and celebrity to kiss and grope women without their consent. "You know I'm automatically attracted to beautiful—I just start kissing them. It's like a magnet. Just kiss. I don't even wait," he said. "And when you're a star, they let you do it, you can do anything ... grab them by the p***y. You can do anything" (Cohen 2017). Following the release of the tape, critics charged that Trump acknowledged committing sexual assault and demanded that he withdraw from the presidential race. Although Trump admitted making the comments and apologized for them, he denied any sexual misconduct and described the taped conversation as "locker-room banter." In the ensuing weeks before the election, however, more than a dozen women came forward to claim that Trump sexually assaulted them. Trump denounced his accusers as liars, claimed that they were conspiring with the Clinton campaign to discredit him, and implied that several of the women were not attractive enough to interest him.

As the November election approached, Trump and Clinton faced off in a series of three televised debates. Critics described Trump's behavior toward Clinton during the debates as sexist, bullying, and patronizing. In the first debate, Trump interrupted the Democratic nominee 25 times in the first 26 minutes and frequently talked over her. During the second debate, which featured a town-hall format, Trump often stood close behind Clinton while she was talking, as if to intimidate her with his physical presence. "We were on a small stage and no matter where I walked, he followed me closely, staring at me, making faces," Clinton recalled in her 2017 memoir *What Happened.* "It was incredibly uncomfortable. He was literally breathing down my neck. My skin crawled." During the third debate, as Clinton discussed her proposal to increase Social Security contributions for wealthy Americans, including her opponent, Trump dismissively responded, "Such a nasty woman" (Cohen 2017). Clinton's supporters quickly adopted "nasty woman" as a badge of honor and put the phrase on T-shirts and campaign signs.

Impact on the Election

Although Trump's behavior toward women generated tremendous controversy, it did not end up costing him the election. Voters who cast their ballots for him either dismissed the allegations as untrue or decided that his conduct did not disqualify him from serving as president. In fact, polls suggested that the sexist views Trump expressed during the campaign were not out of line with those held by many Americans. A survey conducted in April 2016 found that 42 percent of Americans—and 68 percent of Trump supporters—agreed that the United States had become "too soft and feminine." Respondents who agreed with the statement were four times more likely to hold a "very unfavorable" opinion of Clinton than those who disagreed (Cox 2016). Some researchers concluded that Clinton's candidacy provoked a sexist backlash among members of the electorate who felt threatened by her ambition and rejection of traditional gender roles (Beinart 2016).

Public debate about Trump's alleged sexual misconduct drew attention to the mistreatment of women by other men in positions of power. Several high-profile media personalities who provided extensive coverage of the 2016 presidential campaign were later accused of sexual harassment, including Mark Halperin of ABC News, Matt Lauer of NBC News, Bill O'Reilly of Fox News, and Glenn Thrush of *Politico.* In light of these developments, some observers questioned whether underlying misogynist attitudes pervaded media coverage of the campaign. "The men that told us the story of the 2016 campaigns—who shaped the narrative surrounding one of the most consequential presidential elections in modern history—are the same men who abused their female colleagues," wrote one analyst. "These men told voters which issues they should care about (private email servers) and which they should ignore (Trump's history of treating women like second-class citizens)" (Carreiro 2017).

In the wake of Trump's election, some observers expressed concern that his leadership on the world stage would normalize misogyny and reverse gains toward women's equality. Sharan Burrow, one of seven female cochairs of the World Economic Forum, told CNBC that President Trump "has managed, with the rise of other alpha male leaders, to unleash a wave of misogyny around the world as if it is legitimate in 2018" (Amaro 2018). As allegations of sexual misconduct brought down a series of powerful men in media, politics, and entertainment that year, some of Trump's accusers pursued legal action in an effort to hold him accountable, as well.

Further Reading

Amaro, Silvia. 2018. "WEF Co-Chair Says Trump Has Helped to Unleash a 'Wave of Misogyny.'" CNBC, January 26. https://www.cnbc.com/2018/01/26/wef -co-chair-says-trump-has-helped-to-unleash-of-wave-of-misogyny.html

Associated Press (AP). 2016. "Donald Trump Rated Looks of Contestants on 'The Apprentice.'" *Daily Telegraph*, October 3. https://www.telegraph.co.uk/ news/2016/10/03/donald-trump-rated-looks-of-female-contestants-on-the -apprentice/

Beinart, Peter. 2016. "Fear of a Female President." *Atlantic*, October. https:// www.theatlantic.com/magazine/archive/2016/10/fear-of-a-female-president/ 497564/

Carreiro, Remy A. 2017. "How Misogynistic Male Reporters Shaped the Coverage of the 2016 Election." *Rantt Media*, November 27. https://rantt.com/how -misogynistic-male-reporters-shaped-the-coverage-of-the-2016-election/

Cohen, Claire. 2017. "Donald Trump Sexism Tracker: Every Offensive Comment in One Place." *Daily Telegraph*, July 14. https://www.telegraph.co.uk/ women/politics/donald-trump-sexism-tracker-every-offensive-comment -in-one-place/

Cox, Daniel, and Robert P. Jones. 2016. "Two-Thirds of Trump Supporters Say Nation Needs a Leader Willing to Break the Rules." PRRI/*Atlantic*, April 7. https://www.prri.org/research/prri-atlantic-poll-republican-democratic -primary-trump-supporters/#.V0RtTDese48

Robbins, Mel. 2017. "Hillary Clinton Lost Because of Sexism." CNN, May 3. https://www.cnn.com/2017/05/03/opinions/hillary-clinton-interview -sexism-robbins/index.html

Scott, Eugene. 2018. "White Women Helped Elect Trump. Now He's Losing Their
    Support." *Washington Post*, January 22. https://www.washingtonpost.com/
    news/the-fix/wp/2018/01/22/white-women-helped-elect-trump-now-hes
    -losing-their-support/?utm_term=.d23009b2a313
Tur, Katy. 2017. *Unbelievable: My Front-Row Seat to the Craziest Campaign in
    American History*. New York: Dey Street Books.

The Women's March on Washington (2017)

The largest single-day protest in American history took place on January 21, 2017—one day after the inauguration of Republican businessman Donald Trump (1946–) as the 45th President of the United States. The flagship Women's March in Washington, D.C., attracted more than 500,000 people, while "sister" marches in more than 400 cities and towns across the United States drew an additional 3 million. Counting the participants in more than 150 international marches on all seven continents, the total number of marchers worldwide reached an estimated 5 million (Women's March 2018).

The 2016 presidential election served as the impetus for the Women's March. Millions of women in the United States and around the world had been preparing to celebrate the election of Democratic candidate Hillary Clinton (1947–) as America's first female president. In the weeks before voters cast their ballots on November 8, pollsters and pundits estimated the likelihood of her winning at over 90 percent. Clinton's supporters thus viewed Trump's electoral victory as a shocking upset, which contributed to their feelings of grief and outrage. In addition, Trump made controversial comments about women, racial and ethnic minorities, immigrants, Muslims, and LGBTQ individuals during his campaign. Critics worried that his administration and the Republican-controlled Congress would roll back civil rights protections for these groups and implement policies that would prove detrimental to their welfare.

Although organizers of the Women's March claimed that they did not intend for the demonstration to serve as a direct rebuke of Trump, many people expressed a desire to resist the views and priorities that characterized his campaign. "The rhetoric of the past election cycle has insulted, demonized, and threatened many of us," organizers stated. "In the spirit of democracy and in honor of the champions of human rights, dignity, and justice who have come before us, we join in diversity to show our presence in numbers too great to ignore. The Women's March on Washington will send a bold message to our new administration on their first day in office, and to the world, that women's rights are human rights. We stand together, recognizing that defending the most marginalized among us is defending all of us" (ILRF 2017).

Organizing the March

The original idea for the march came from a Facebook post by Teresa Shook, a retired attorney and grandmother of four from Hawaii. Although Shook had never been involved in politics before, she felt compelled to take action following Trump's victory. "I went to bed the night of the election just discouraged and woke up feeling worse the next day thinking how could this be?" she recalled. "I was just sad and dumbfounded from the rhetoric of the campaign and the hatred and bigotry" (Davis 2017). After expressing her frustrations on Facebook, Shook created an event page and invited her friends who felt the same way to join a protest march in Washington, D.C., on the weekend of Trump's inauguration. To her surprise, the number of responses grew from a few dozen to 10,000 overnight. Other concerned citizens—such as New York fashion designer Bob Bland (1982–)—created similar pages, and the number of people expressing interest quickly exceeded 100,000.

The viral response to the idea of organizing a protest march got the attention of experienced political organizers and national interest groups. The initial grassroots efforts turned into a formal campaign headed by journalist and progressive activist Vanessa Wruble (1974–). She enlisted four national cochairs to ensure that the event represented diverse perspectives and interests: Bland; Tamika D. Mallory (1980–), a black activist and former executive director of the National Action Network; Carmen Perez (1977–), a Latina activist and executive director of The Gathering for Justice; and Linda Sarsour (1980–), a Muslim activist and executive director of the Arab American Association of New York. In a gesture of respect for the women's rights, civil rights, and human rights campaigns of the past, organizers selected Harry Belafonte, Angela Davis, LaDonna Harris, Dolores Huerta, and Gloria Steinem as honorary cochairs. More than 400 organizations focusing on various progressive causes signed on as official partners for the Women's March, including Planned Parenthood, the National Resources Defense Council, the National Association for the Advancement of Colored People (NAACP), the League of Women Voters, the National Center for Lesbian Rights, and the American Indian Movement.

On the day of the march, people descended on Washington from all across the country, arriving via air, rail, private vehicles, and chartered buses. Participants represented a wide variety of ages, races, ethnicities, gender identities, and walks of life. For many, the march marked their first foray into political activism. Large numbers of protesters wore pink knitted hats with pointed ears, known as "p***yhats," to signify their objection to Trump's comments on the infamous 2005 *Access Hollywood* tape, when he appeared to boast about groping women's genitals. Many others wore T-shirts or carried signs expressing support for progressive causes that impacted women, such as abortion rights, maternity leave, affordable health care, equal pay, immigration reform, gun control, police violence, and environmental protection. Many marchers chanted the slogan "women's rights are human rights," which Clinton first used in a 1995 speech.

The Women's March on Washington started on Independence Avenue near the Capitol Building and proceeded along the National Mall. A series of prominent speakers addressed the crowd, articulating messages that ranged from compassion and camaraderie to determination and defiance. "Our constitution does not begin with 'I, the President.' It begins with, 'We, the People,' " said feminist icon Gloria Steinem. "I am proud to be one of thousands who have come to Washington to make clear that we will keep working for a democracy in which we are linked as human beings, not ranked by race or gender or class or any other label." Actress and activist America Ferrara noted that "Our dignity, our character, our rights have all been under attack, and a platform of hate and division assumed power yesterday. But the president is not America. His cabinet is not America. Congress is not America. We are America. And we are here to stay." Singer Alicia Keys added that "We will not allow our bodies to be owned and controlled by men in government or any men anywhere for that matter. We will not allow our compassionate souls to get stepped on. We want the best for all Americans. No hate. No bigotry. No Muslim registry. We value education, healthcare, and equality" (Lindig 2017).

Political Impact

Trump tweeted a defiant response to the Women's March the following morning. "Watched protests yesterday but was under the impression that we just had an election! Why didn't these people vote?" he wrote. Less than two hours later, however, he adopted a more conciliatory tone in a second tweet: "Peaceful protests are a hallmark of our democracy. Even if I don't always agree, I recognize the rights of people to express their views" (Lerer 2017). Conservative critics largely dismissed the march as a one-time expression of frustration by liberals whose preferred candidate had failed to win the election. Although organizers acknowledged that the demonstrations might not have a measurable impact on the Trump administration's agenda, they expressed hope that participants in the march would launch a wave of activism in their communities upon returning home. "Women are angry, and women are getting involved, and that's the key, that this march mobilized women and that they work with the anger and use it and don't let it drop," political historian Jean Harris told *USA Today* (Przybyla 2017).

Some women who felt energized by the Women's March decided that the best way to eliminate sexism from politics was to run for office. According to the Center for American Women and Politics, a record number of women launched political campaigns in 2017, including 390 candidates for the U.S. House of Representatives and 79 candidates for state governorships. This trend surprised some political observers, who predicted that Clinton's defeat would dampen women's enthusiasm for entering the political arena. To support female candidates and amplify women's voices in politics, Women's March organizers launched a nationwide voter-registration initiative called Power to the Polls. Empowered by their new-found political awareness, activists who participated in the march sent 250,000 postcards to senators in a successful effort to prevent repeal of the Affordable Care Act (Chira 2017).

Further Reading

Chira, Susan. 2018. "The Women's March Became a Movement. What's Next?" *New York Times*, January 20. https://www.nytimes.com/2018/01/20/us/womens-march-metoo.html

Chozick, Amy. 2018. "Hillary Clinton Ignited a Feminist Movement. By Losing." *New York Times*, January 13. https://www.nytimes.com/2018/01/13/sunday-review/hillary-clinton-feminist-movement.html

Davis, Chelsea. 2017. "Maui Woman Starts What Could Be Largest Trump Inauguration Movement." *Hawaii News Now*, January 6. http://www.hawaiinewsnow.com/story/34198283/maui-woman-starts-what-could-be-largest-trump-inauguration-movement

International Labor Rights Forum (ILRF). 2017. "Women's March on Washington." https://www.laborrights.org/events/women%E2%80%99s-march-washington

Lerer, Lisa, and Jonathan Lemire. 2017. "Trump Offers Scattershot Response to Global Women's March." PBS, January 22. https://www.pbs.org/newshour/politics/trump-response-womens-march

Lindig, Sarah. 2017. "The Most Inspiring Quotes from the Women's March Speeches." *Elle*, January 21. https://www.elle.com/culture/career-politics/news/a42344/inspiring-quotes-womens-march-speeches/

Przybyla, Heidi M. 2017. "Women's March an 'Entry Point' for New Activist Wave." *USA Today*, January 5. https://www.usatoday.com/story/news/politics/2017/01/05/womens-march-searches-themes-amid-concern-trump-gop-congress/96199000/

Women's March. 2018. "The March." https://www.womensmarch.com/march/
Women's March Organizers. 2018. *Together We Rise: The Women's March.*
    New York: HarperCollins.

The Harvey Weinstein Scandal (2017)

During the 2016 presidential campaign, more than a dozen women accused Republican candidate Donald Trump (1946–) of sexual misconduct. When voters elected him president despite these allegations, some observers predicted that the apparent lack of public concern would make women reluctant to come forward with such complaints in the future. Instead, the idea that powerful men could take advantage of their positions to abuse women generated a sense of outrage that seemed to imbue more women with the courage to make public disclosures. Over the next year, a series of prominent men in the worlds of media, politics, and entertainment faced new accusations of sexual harassment or assault.

Some of the most shocking allegations surrounded film industry executive Harvey Weinstein (1952–). As the cofounder and longtime head of Miramax and the Weinstein Company (TWC), Weinstein built a reputation as one of the most successful and influential producers in Hollywood. Films produced by Weinstein's companies—including *Pulp Fiction* (1994), *The English Patient* (1996), *Good Will Hunting* (1997), *Shakespeare in Love* (1998), and *The King's Speech* (2010)—collected more than 300 Academy Award nominations, won Best Picture honors six times, and launched the careers of countless stars. Weinstein also made his mark in politics as a prolific fundraiser for Democratic candidates and a champion of liberal causes, including women's rights.

The New York Times Publishes Allegations

On October 5, 2017, the *New York Times* published an investigative report detailing allegations of sexual misconduct against Weinstein spanning nearly 30 years. Many of the complaints involved young, aspiring actresses and models who attended what they thought were professional meetings to discuss career opportunities, only to be subjected to unwanted sexual advances by the powerful producer. The women claimed that Weinstein engaged in a pattern of predatory behavior that included requesting massages, asking them to watch him shower, exposing himself, masturbating in front of them, groping them, or raping them. Many alleged victims described their experiences with Weinstein as an exploitive "casting couch" situation, in which they felt obligated or coerced to provide sexual favors in exchange for career advancement.

Some claimed that Weinstein threatened to withhold opportunities or derail their careers if they rejected his advances.

New York Times reporters Jodi Kantor and Megan Twohey interviewed employees of Weinstein's film enterprises and obtained legal documents and correspondence. They presented evidence suggesting that Weinstein went to great lengths to cover up charges of sexual misconduct over the years, including paying financial settlements to at least eight women between 1990 and 2015. In 1997, for instance, he paid $100,000 to Rose McGowan (1973–), a 23-year-old actress who appeared in the movie *Scream* (1996). The agreement specified that the payment did not constitute an admission of guilt by Weinstein, and that it was only intended to avoid litigation and stave off negative publicity. Once the article appeared, McGowan emerged as one of Weinstein's most vocal critics. On Twitter, she accused the producer of raping her in a hotel room during the Sundance Film Festival and asserted that others in the film industry were complicit because they had known about her experience.

Weinstein immediately responded to the allegations in a statement to the *New York Times*. He noted that the rules of appropriate conduct in the workplace changed during his long tenure in the film industry, and he acknowledged that "the way I've behaved with colleagues in the past has caused a lot of pain, and I sincerely apologize for it. Though I'm trying to do better, I know I have a long way to go." Describing the situation as a "wake-up call," Weinstein outlined his plan to take a leave of absence and undergo therapy in an effort to "conquer my demons." He also mentioned some of the initiatives he sponsored to support women in Hollywood and expressed his desire to earn "a second chance in the community" (Kantor and Twohey 2017). Weinstein's attorney also issued a statement, however, saying that the producer unequivocally denied all allegations of nonconsensual sex and retaliation against women who refused his advances.

On October 10, journalist Ronan Farrow published an article in the *New Yorker* that included accusations against Weinstein made by 13 more women. The article also featured information from TWC employees who claimed to have witnessed or facilitated Weinstein's meetings with young women. "He would have them late at night, usually at hotel bars or in hotel rooms. And, in order to make these women feel more comfortable, he would ask a female executive or assistant to start those meetings with him," said one employee. "It almost felt like the executive or assistant was made to be a honeypot to lure these women in, to make them feel safe. Then he would dismiss the executive or the assistant, and then these women were alone with him. And that did not feel like it was appropriate behavior or safe behavior" (Farrow 2017). On occasions when young actresses appeared upset when they emerged from such meetings, the employees were expected to calm them down. Although some TWC employees expressed regret or shame about their role in the meetings, their employment contracts included clauses that forbade them from criticizing the company publicly or harming the reputation of its management.

The Scandal Rocks Hollywood

In the ensuing weeks, 85 women came forward to accuse Weinstein of sexual harassment or unwanted physical contact. The list of accusers included some of the biggest names in Hollywood, such as Ashley Judd, Gwyneth Paltrow, Angelina Jolie, Darryl Hannah, Uma Thurman, Annabella Sciorra, Rosanna Arquette, Mira Sorvino, Lupita Nyong'o, and Salma Hayek. Hayek claimed that Weinstein threatened to shut down production of *Frida* (2002), a film that she described as her "greatest ambition" to make, unless she agreed to shoot a sex scene with another woman. "And he demanded full-frontal nudity," she wrote in the *New York Times*. "It was clear to me he would never let me finish this movie without him having his fantasy one way or another. There was no room for negotiation. I had to say yes" (Hayek 2017). Arquette claimed that Weinstein blacklisted her in Hollywood after she rebuffed his advances, damaging her career for years.

As the scandal spread, some critics questioned why the women waited so long to come forward. Some accusers attributed their reluctance to the power dynamics in the film industry, where prominent studio executives like Weinstein exerted control over scripts, roles, projects, funding, and media coverage. They decided that exposing his behavior would destroy their acting careers, so they kept quiet in the interest of preserving the professional relationship. Some reported feeling embarrassed, ashamed, intimidated, or afraid that no one would believe them. In 2015, model Ambra Battilana Gutierrez (1993–) went straight to New York City police following a meeting with Weinstein in which she claimed he grabbed her breasts and put his hand up her skirt. Police detectives arranged for her to wear a wire and secretly record a conversation in which Weinstein admitted touching her inappropriately. Despite her efforts, the district attorney declined to press criminal charges against him.

As the allegations mounted, however, the balance of power shifted to the women who accused Weinstein of sexual misconduct. In late 2017 and early 2018, the producer faced a series of personal, professional, and legal repercussions. His wife, fashion designer Georgina Chapman, announced that she was filing for divorce. Following an internal inquiry, the board of directors at TWC announced that Weinstein had been fired from the company. The Producers Guild, the British Academy of Film and Television Arts (BAFTA), and the Academy of Motion Picture Arts and Sciences all revoked Weinstein's membership. In May 2018, Weinstein was indicted on criminal charges in New York City stemming from rape allegations, prompting a flurry of celebratory social media posts by his accusers. "I, and so many of Harvey Weinstein's survivors, had given up hope that our rapist would be held accountable by law," McGowan wrote on Instagram. "May his arrest give hope to all victims and survivors everywhere that are telling their truths" (McGowan 2018).

Further Reading

BBC News. 2018. "Harvey Weinstein Timeline: How the Scandal Unfolded." February 12. http://www.bbc.com/news/entertainment-arts-41594672

Farrow, Ronan. 2017. "From Aggressive Overtures to Sexual Assault: Harvey Weinstein's Accusers Tell Their Stories." *New Yorker*, October 23. https://www.newyorker.com/news/news-desk/from-aggressive-overtures-to-sexual-assault-harvey-weinsteins-accusers-tell-their-stories

Hayek, Salma. 2017. "Harvey Weinstein Was My Monster Too." *New York Times*, December 12. https://www.nytimes.com/interactive/2017/12/13/opinion/contributors/salma-hayek-harvey-weinstein.html

Kantor, Jodi, and Megan Twohey. 2017. "Harvey Weinstein Paid Off Sexual Harassment Accusers for Decades." *New York Times*, October 5. https://www.nytimes.com/2017/10/05/us/harvey-weinstein-harassment-allegations.html?_r=0

McGowan, Rose. 2018. Instagram post, May 24. https://www.instagram.com/p/BjLRgGRAzuJ/?hl=en&taken-by=rosemcgowan

Alyssa Milano's #MeToo Tweet (2017)

In October 2017, dozens of female celebrities came forward to accuse Hollywood film producer Harvey Weinstein (1952–) of predatory sexual behavior, ranging from harassment to groping to rape. In what became known as the "Weinstein effect," these allegations produced a tidal wave of sexual misconduct charges against other powerful men in the worlds of media, entertainment, and politics. By the end of January 2018, more than 150 high-profile men had been publicly accused, including filmmakers James Toback and Brett Ratner, actors Louis C. K. and Kevin Spacey, television journalists Matt Lauer and Charlie Rose, U.S. Congressmen Al Franken and John Conyers, and celebrity chefs Mario Batali and John Besh. The disclosures tarnished the men's reputations or ended their careers.

Prior to the Weinstein scandal, many women quietly endured indignities and abuse by high-ranking men in the workplace. Shame and embarrassment, fear of retaliation, and concern that authorities would dismiss their complaints prevented many women from reporting sexual harassment. When a parade of famous women spoke out against Weinstein, however, it prompted a national reassessment of how sexual harassment claims were viewed and handled. Millions of women gained the courage to share their own experiences, offer support to survivors of sexual abuse, and denounce sexual offenders.

Much of the credit for the shift in public attitudes belongs to the #MeToo movement, a social media campaign aimed at supporting survivors of sexual misconduct. The activist and actress Alyssa Milano (1972–) popularized the phrase on October 15, 2017, and it quickly became a rallying cry for women around the world. Milano's message featured a screenshot from a friend suggesting that "If all the women who have been sexually harassed or assaulted wrote 'Me Too' as a status, we might give people a sense of the magnitude of the problem." Milano added, "If you've been sexually harassed or assaulted, write 'Me Too' as a reply to this tweet." Within 24 hours, 500,000 people responded on Twitter, and the hashtag #MeToo appeared on Facebook 12 million times (CBS 2017). Many celebrities lent their voices to the conversation by acknowledging that they had experienced sexual harassment or assault, including Sheryl Crow, Viola Davis, Rosario Dawson, America Ferrara, Lady Gaga, Debra Messing, Anna Paquin, Molly Ringwald, Uma Thurman, and Gabrielle Union.

Activists Raise Awareness of Sexual Violence

Milano became a teen idol through her starring role as Tony Danza's daughter Samantha on the popular sitcom *Who's the Boss* (1984–1992). She went on to costar with Rose McGowan on *Charmed* (1998–2006), a hit fantasy-drama series about three witches who used their powers for good. She also supported charitable causes and spoke out on issues that mattered to her. She served as a UNICEF ambassador, wore a dress made of vegetables in an advertisement for People for the Ethical Treatment of Animals (PETA), raised money to provide clean water for people in developing countries through Charity: Water, and publicly discussed her struggles with postpartum anxiety and depression to help eliminate the stigma surrounding mental illness. As social media emerged, Milano took full advantage of the platform to educate and inspire her fans. When she saw her friend's tweet about sexual harassment at the height of the Weinstein scandal, she immediately passed it along to her 3 million Twitter followers. "I thought, you know what? This is an amazing way to get some idea of the magnitude of how big this problem is," she recalled. "It was also a way to get the focus off these horrible men and to put the focus back on the victims and survivors" (Sayej 2017).

Milano had no idea that her #MeToo tweet would go viral and launch an international movement. At the time she posted it, she was also unaware that the phrase "Me Too" had been coined in 2006—before the widespread adoption of social media—by the African American civil rights activist Tarana Burke (1973–). Burke met a 13-year-old girl who confided that she had been sexually assaulted by her mother's boyfriend. In the moment, Burke struggled to come up with an appropriate response to express support for the girl and let her know that she was not alone. As a survivor of sexual abuse herself, Burke later realized that she could have provided a powerful message of "empowerment through empathy" by simply saying, "Me too." She turned it into the catchphrase for a grassroots campaign to promote healing for women of color who had experienced sexual violence or exploitation.

A number of Twitter users responded to Milano's #MeToo tweet by pointing out that Burke had been using the phrase for more than a decade. Some expressed irritation that the media inadvertently attributed it to Milano. Burke acknowledged that she initially felt upset when the hashtag suddenly began trending on social media. "I felt a sense of dread," she noted, "because something that was part of my life's work was going to be co-opted and taken from me and used for a purpose that I hadn't originally intended" (Garcia 2017). Milano quickly corrected the mistake and publicly credited Burke as the original founder of the movement. "I was just made aware of an earlier #MeToo movement," she wrote on Twitter, "and the origin story is equal parts heartbreaking and inspiring" (Leah 2017).

Given Burke's long history of helping women of color who had experienced sexual violence, some supporters questioned why the #MeToo movement only gained traction after Milano and other celebrities came forward. "In a perfect world, people would just care and would want to see this situation elevated to public issue, but that's just not the reality that we live in," Burke stated. "We are a society that thrives off of celebrity culture, so it always takes something to break the ice, and if it takes celebrities coming forward, for me, I don't have time to be annoyed that it didn't happen in a different way.... I'm just happy that it happened" (Wagmeister 2018).

#MeToo Becomes a Global Movement

The #MeToo hashtag launched a global conversation about sexual violence. "It was the perfect storm to happen and I feel really blessed I was the vessel, the messenger," Milano said (Sayej 2017). As millions of women used #MeToo to tell their stories, it built a community of survivors. Milano and Burke worked together to amplify survivors' voices and give them access to resources to promote healing. The movement "is bigger than me and bigger than Alyssa Milano," Burke stated. "Neither one of us should be centered in this work. This is about survivors" (Garcia 2017).

The #MeToo movement encountered a backlash to its mission of exposing the pervasiveness of sexual violence and holding abusers accountable. Critics expressed concern that the sudden cultural shift prompted by the movement created uncertainty and confusion about the boundaries of acceptable behavior. They worried that #MeToo would lead to men being accused of sexual harassment based on awkward attempts at flirting or mildly sexist humor, with severe repercussions for their reputations or careers. Some critics also asserted that #MeToo might encourage women to make false allegations in order to join the movement. #MeToo activists rejected these criticisms, arguing that most survivors found it so arduous to come forward with sexual harassment claims that they never told their stories. They noted that #MeToo provided a safe environment for survivors to receive support without sharing traumatic personal experiences. "That's what #MeToo is—you don't have to tell your story," Milano explained. "You just have to say, 'me too' " (Sayej 2017).

Further Reading

CBS Interactive. 2017. "More Than 12 Million 'Me Too' Facebook Posts, Comments, Reactions in 24 Hours." CBS News, October 17. https://www.cbsnews.com/news/metoo-more-than-12-million-facebook-posts-comments-reactions-24-hours/

Garcia, Sandra E. 2017. "The Woman Who Created #MeToo Long before Hashtags." *New York Times*, October 20. https://www.nytimes.com/2017/10/20/us/me-too-movement-tarana-burke.html

Leah, Rachel. 2017. "Hollywood's Brightest Join the Ten-Year-Old #MeToo Movement, but Will That Change Anything?" *Salon*, October 17. https://www.salon.com/2017/10/17/metoo-tarana-burke-jennifer-lawrence/

Sayej, Nadja. 2017. "Alyssa Milano on the #MeToo Movement: 'We're Not Going to Stand for It Anymore.'" *Guardian*, December 1. https://www.theguardian.com/culture/2017/dec/01/alyssa-milano-mee-too-sexual-harassment-abuse

Wagmeister, Elizabeth. 2018. "Tarana Burke on Hollywood, Time's Up, and Me Too Backlash." *Variety*, April 10. http://variety.com/2018/biz/news/tarana-burke-times-up-me-too-backlash-1202748822/

Time Magazine Recognizes the "Silence Breakers" (2017)

Since 1927, *Time* magazine has produced a special issue recognizing the person, group, or idea that most influenced news or events for that year. In 2017, the editors chose the "Silence Breakers"—women who spoke out against sexual harassment and launched the #MeToo movement—as the magazine's annual Person of the Year. *Time* editor in chief Edward Felsenthal recognized the group "for giving voice to open secrets, for moving whisper networks onto social networks, for pushing us all to stop accepting the unacceptable" (Felsenthal 2017).

The cover of the December 18 issue featured a portrait of five women who took public stands against sexual harassment: actress Ashley Judd, one of the first to come forward with allegations against Hollywood producer Harvey Weinstein (1952–); singer Taylor Swift (1989–), who testified in court about being groped by a Denver disc jockey; Uber engineer Susan Fowler (1990?–), who blew the whistle on pervasive sexual harassment in the technology industry; lobbyist Adama Iwu, who started a campaign to expose sexual harassment in the California legislature; and agricultural worker Isabel Pascual, who spoke out against sexual misconduct by a supervisor. The cover also included the elbow of an unidentified woman to represent victims who had yet to come forward. "This is the fastest-moving social change we've seen in decades," Felsenthal said, "and it began with individual acts of courage by hundreds of women, and some men, who came forward to tell their own stories of sexual harassment and assault" (May 2017).

A Cultural Shift

In tracing the shift in public attitudes toward sexual harassment, some observers claimed that the change took root during the 2016 presidential election campaign. Many women objected to what they viewed as sexist remarks and behavior by Republican candidate Donald Trump (1946–), including a videotaped conversation from a 2005 appearance on *Access Hollywood* in which Trump seemingly boasted about sexually assaulting women. When voters elected Trump president over Democratic candidate Hillary Clinton (1947–)—the first female presidential nominee from a major political party—many women interpreted it as the electorate demonstrating a lack of concern about sexual violence. "I think that President Trump's election in many ways was a setback for women," said Megyn Kelly, a journalist featured among *Time*'s Silence Breakers for raising concerns about sexual harassment by Fox News executives. "The overall message to us was that we don't really matter" (Zacharek 2017).

The so-called Weinstein effect was another precipitating factor in changing societal views of sexual misconduct. In an online survey conducted by *Time* in late November 2017—around six weeks after Judd and a succession of other celebrities made allegations against the film producer—82 percent of respondents said the Weinstein scandal made women more likely to report sexual harassment (Zacharek 2017). "Women everywhere have begun to speak out about the inappropriate, abusive, and in some cases illegal behavior they've faced," *Time* noted about the revolution ignited by the Silence Breakers. "When a movie star says #MeToo, it becomes easier to believe the cook who's been quietly enduring for years" (Zacharek 2017).

In addition to Weinstein accusers like Judd and Rose McGowan (1973–), the Person of the Year issue also featured Tarana Burke (1973–), the activist who coined the term "Me Too" in 2006, and Alyssa Milano (1972–), the activist who popularized the #MeToo hashtag in the wake of the Weinstein scandal. The issue also told the stories of dozens of ordinary women from various industries who had experienced unwanted sexual advances in the workplace. Several of the women preferred to remain anonymous because they worried that complaining publicly would lead to retaliation or being fired from their jobs. "As much as the stigma around this has been removed this year because of the Me Too movement, it's still really difficult for a lot of women to come forward," *Time* national correspondent Charlotte Alter stated. "It's important to include people who have to stay anonymous for professional reasons, who don't have the resources to weather what would happen if they lost their job or they couldn't support their families. So we wanted to include [these people] to really reference the risk that these women are taking by speaking out about this" (Mallon 2017).

Time's Person of the Year cover story commended the Silence Breakers for having the courage to come forward despite the risks. It praised the individuals profiled for raising awareness of the pervasiveness of sexual harassment, forging a sense of solidarity among survivors of sexual abuse, and creating an environment where sexual misconduct will no longer be tolerated. The next step, according to #MeToo activists, will involve dismantling the male-dominated workplace power structure that allowed the problem to develop. As a step in that direction, according to Alter, women conceived, wrote, designed, and produced the 2017 Person of the Year cover, article, and online video.

Although many readers praised *Time* for recognizing the emerging movement to end sexual violence, some critics objected to the term "Silence Breakers" to describe the activists profiled. They argued that victims of sexual harassment did not necessarily stay silent before the wave of celebrity revelations launched the #MeToo movement. Many ordinary working women came forward, only to see their complaints ignored or dismissed. In addition, some feminists pointed out that *Time* had only recognized four individual women in the nine-decade history of its Person of the Year issue. When the magazine recognized female newsmakers, it usually featured them as part of a group, while many deserving women never saw their accomplishments acknowledged. Finally, some readers criticized *Time* for including Trump on the list of runners up for its 2017 Person of the Year. Given that more than a dozen women have accused Trump of sexual harassment or assault, critics charged that his inclusion detracted from the magazine's choice of the Silence Breakers.

Further Reading

Felsenthal, Edward. 2017. "*Time* Person of the Year: The Choice." *Time*, December 18. http://time.com/time-person-of-the-year-2017-silence-breakers-choice/

Mallon, Maggie. 2017. "There's a Powerful Hidden Message on *Time* Magazine's Person of the Year Cover." *Glamour*, December 6. https://www.glamour.com/story/hidden-message-in-time-magazine-person-of-the-year-2017-cover#intcid=recommendations_default-similar2_ceb17a0e-7b5c-45ee-9c35-880350fb5fcd_cral2-1

May, Ashley. 2017. "Who Are the Silence Breakers Featured as Time Person of the Year?" *USA Today*, December 6. https://www.usatoday.com/story/life/nation-now/2017/12/06/who-silence-breakers-featured-time-person-year-me-too/926243001/

Zacharek, Stephanie, Eliana Dockterman, and Haley Sweetland Edwards. 2017. "*Time* Person of the Year 2017: The Silence Breakers." *Time*, December 18. http://time.com/time-person-of-the-year-2017-silence-breakers/

Dr. Larry Nassar Is Convicted of Sexually Abusing Athletes (2018)

The #MeToo reckoning shook the world of elite sports in 2017, when USA Gymnastics national team doctor and Michigan State University osteopathic physician Larry Nassar (1963–) pleaded guilty to criminal sexual conduct involving young female athletes. Around 300 girls and women accused Nassar of sexually abusing them during medical treatments, including such decorated U.S. Olympians as Simone Biles, Gabby Douglas, McKayla Maroney, and Aly Raisman. In January 2018, more than 150 of Nassar's victims took advantage of the opportunity to confront him publicly during the sentencing phase of his trial. The strength, courage, and resilience displayed by this "army of survivors" generated widespread public support for the #MeToo movement. The Nassar scandal also raised pointed questions about the failure of nationally prominent institutions to keep young athletes safe and respond promptly to allegations of sexual abuse.

Abuse Disguised as Medical Treatment

Nassar first became involved with USA Gymnastics as an athletic trainer in 1986. He went on to become the team doctor and national medical co-ordinator after earning a degree from the College of Osteopathic Medicine at Michigan State University in 1993. Nassar cemented his reputation as a leading sports-medicine physician during the 1996 Olympic Games. When American gymnast Kerri Strug sprained her ankle on a vault, Nassar provided treatment that enabled Strug to complete a second vault and help the U.S. team clinch a gold medal. Afterward, he became an assistant professor at MSU's medical school and published academic papers on the treatment of gymnastics injuries.

From the mid-1990s onward, Nassar treated gymnasts and other athletes at the MSU sports medicine clinic, USA Gymnastics training camps, the Karolyi Ranch in Texas, and the Twistars Gymnastics Club in Lansing, Michigan. Many young gymnasts found him to be a kind and supportive presence in the pressure-packed environment of elite gymnastics. He often gave girls candy or trinkets from his Olympic experiences and listened sympathetically to their complaints about tough coaches and intense workouts. "He was always that person who would stick up for me," Raisman recalled. "The more I think about it, the more I realize how twisted he was, how he manipulated me to make me think that he had my back when he didn't" (Kirby 2018).

Nassar took advantage of his patients' trust and his status as a recognized expert to commit serial sexual molestation under the guise of medical treatment. He regularly massaged patients' buttocks and breasts and inserted his fingers into their vaginas. He claimed that the digital penetration was a legitimate form of osteopathic manipulation of the joints, muscles, and ligaments. In fact, some doctors do perform intravaginal procedures to treat chronic pain, bladder leakage, and other health issues related to the pelvic floor. Nassar routinely used the technique on patients whose injuries did not involve the pelvis, however, and he broke professional guidelines by not wearing gloves, not explaining the rationale behind the procedures, not obtaining patient consent, and not having a nurse, parent, or other chaperone present in the room.

Although many patients acknowledged that Nassar's treatments made them feel uncomfortable, most deferred to his authority as a doctor and believed his assertions that intravaginal procedures were medically indicated. On the few occasions when a patient filed a complaint, Nassar managed to deceive investigators. In 2004, for instance, Lansing-area teen Brianne Randall-Gay told Meridian Township Police that Nassar had touched her inappropriately during an appointment. Officers dropped the matter after Nassar showed them a PowerPoint presentation about intravaginal procedures. In 2014, recent MSU graduate Amanda Thomashow told university police that Nassar sexually molested her during a treatment for hip pain. Although her complaint led to a Title IX investigation, MSU cleared Nassar of wrongdoing on the advice of four of his colleagues, who claimed that Thomashow had failed to understand the "nuanced difference" between a medical procedure and sexual abuse.

USA Gymnastics quietly severed ties with Nassar in 2015, after a national team coach raised concerns about his treatment methods. Coach Sarah Jantzi happened to overhear one of her gymnasts, Maggie Nichols, talking to a teammate about Nassar's questionable behavior during a treatment for back pain. "He started touching me in places I really didn't think he should. *I accepted what he was doing because I was told by adults that he was the best doctor and he could help relieve my pain,*" Nichols recalled. "After hearing our conversation, [Jantzi] asked me more questions about it and said it doesn't seem right" (Barr 2018). The coach reported Nassar to USA Gymnastics officials and also informed the athlete's parents. USA Gymnastics promised to take appropriate action and dissuaded the Nichols family from discussing the matter publicly. Although officials filed a report with the Federal Bureau of Investigation, they did not inform MSU of the allegations against Nassar, and they allowed him to say that he had left his position as team doctor voluntarily.

In August 2016, the *Indianapolis Star* published a story about sexual abuse in the world of elite gymnastics. After the story appeared, former gymnast Rachael Denhollander contacted the *Star* to express concern about treatments she had received from the famed physician a decade earlier. "This isn't something I want to do," Denhollander said of coming forward. "I was ashamed. I was very embarrassed. And I was very confused, trying to reconcile what was happening with the person he was supposed to be. He's this famous doctor. He's trusted by my friends. He's trusted by these other gymnasts. How could he reach this position in the medical profession, how could he reach this kind of prominence and stature if this is who he is?" (Evans 2016). On September 12, the *Star* published a new story focusing on the allegations surrounding Nassar, in which he denied performing intravaginal procedures on patients. The report prompted a wave of outraged calls from former patients demanding to know why Nassar was suddenly disavowing what he had always claimed was a legitimate medical technique.

Fallout from the Sex Abuse Scandal

MSU responded to the allegations against Nassar by terminating his employment at the sports medicine clinic and notifying the police. Another young woman, Kyle Stephens, came forward to accuse Nassar of repeatedly sexually molesting her in the basement of his home beginning in 1998, when she was six years old. Although she told her parents about the abuse a few years later, they were friends of Nassar and believed the doctor's denials. Stephens's allegations helped police investigators circumvent Nassar's medical defense, since the abuse had not occurred as part of a treatment. Police obtained a warrant to search Nassar's home, where they found more than 37,000 images of child pornography on his computer. In December 2016, Nassar was arrested on state charges of first-degree criminal sexual assault of a minor child as well as federal child pornography charges.

Over the next few months, dozens of other women came forward to accuse Nassar of sexual abuse, including several well-known Olympic gymnasts. Many gained courage from the #MeToo movement that arose in the wake of celebrity allegations of sexual misconduct against Hollywood movie producer Harvey Weinstein. Nassar pleaded guilty to the child pornography charges in July 2017 and received a sentence of 60 years in federal prison. In November 2017, he pleaded guilty to 10 counts of first-degree criminal sexual conduct involving sexual penetration of minors. During the sentencing phase of the trial, Ingham County Circuit Court Judge Rosemarie Aquilina agreed to let the survivors of Nassar's abuse address the court. Nassar begged the judge to reconsider, claiming in a six-page letter that it would create a "media circus" and harm his mental health. Aquilina dismissed his objections and allowed the testimony to proceed. "You may find it harsh that you are here listening," she stated. "But nothing is as harsh as what your victims endured for thousands of hours at your hands" (Murphy 2018).

A total of 156 women spoke over seven days in January 2018, sharing tragic stories of abuse, angry words of retribution, and powerful messages of strength and healing. "Perhaps you have figured it out by now, but little girls don't stay little forever," Stephens told Nassar in her victim impact statement. "They grow into strong women that return to destroy your world." "You chose the wrong prey," added former MSU gymnast Larissa Boyce. "We are athletes. We will not give up or give in. We are trained to fight past the pain and hurt. United we are now, an army of amazing women who are paving the path to justice and change" (Mencarini 2018). The powerful testimony garnered widespread praise from political leaders and celebrities and emboldened many more victims of sexual abuse to come forward. When it concluded, Nassar received sentences of 40–175 years and 40–125 years in a Michigan state prison, ensuring that he would remain incarcerated for the rest of his life.

Following Nassar's conviction, public attention shifted to the officials and institutions that failed to recognize his criminal activities and protect his victims from sexual abuse. Critics charged that MSU, USA Gymnastics, Twistars, and other organizations were either negligent or complicit in Nassar's crimes. Several of Nassar's victims asserted that they had complained to coaches or other officials, only to have their allegations ignored or dismissed. The scandal led to the resignation of U.S. Olympic Committee chief executive Scott Blackmun, all 18 members of the USA Gymnastics board of directors, MSU president Lou Anna Simon, MSU athletic director Mark Hollis, and MSU gymnastics coach Kathy Klages. In May 2018, the MSU Board of Regents agreed to pay $500 million to settle lawsuits filed by 332 former patients of Nassar, while numerous lawsuits against USA Gymnastics and other organizations were still pending.

The Nassar investigation also resulted in criminal charges against William Strampel, former dean of the MSU College of Osteopathic Medicine. As Nassar's boss, Strampel was responsible for enforcing changes in treatment protocol that the university imposed after it received complaints about Nassar in 2014. Because Strampel never followed up to make sure Nassar wore gloves, explained his actions to patients, or had a chaperone present when treating "sensitive areas" of the body, Nassar was able to continue assaulting patients for two more years. In addition to neglect of duty for his handling of the Nassar case, Strampel faced charges of harassing, demeaning, propositioning, and soliciting nude photographs from female MSU students. Following a preliminary hearing, a judge determined that there was enough evidence for Strampel to stand trial in June 2018. Strampel also resigned from his tenured position at MSU.

Further Reading

Barr, John. 2018. "Gymnast Maggie Nichols Writes in Letter She Was First to Alert USA Gymnastics to Abuse by Larry Nassar." ESPN, January 9. http://www.espn.com/olympics/story/_/id/22011755/gymnast-maggie-nichols-says-was-first-alert-usa-gymnastics-abuse-larry-nassar

Evans, Tim, Mark Alesia, and Marisa Kwiatkowski. 2016. "Former USA Gymnastics Doctor Accused of Abuse." *Indianapolis Star*, September 12.

https://www.indystar.com/story/news/2016/09/12/former-usa-gymnastics
-doctor-accused-abuse/89995734/

Kirby, Jen. 2018. "The Sex Abuse Scandal Surrounding USA Gymnastics
Team Doctor Larry Nassar, Explained." *Vox*, May 16. https://
www.vox.com/identities/2018/1/19/16897722/sexual-abuse-usa-gymnastics
-larry-nassar-explained

Mencarini, Matt. 2018. "Inside the Investigation and Prosecution of Larry Nassar."
Lansing State Journal, April 5. https://www.lansingstatejournal.com/story/
news/local/2018/04/05/larry-nassar-inside-prosecution-investigation/
472506002/

Murphy, Dan. 2018. "Michigan Judge Dismisses Complaints Made by Larry Nassar
about His Sentencing Hearing." ESPN, January 18. http://www.espn.com/
olympics/story/_/id/22143482/larry-nassar-writes-letter-judge-complaining
-sentencing-hearing

Launch of the Time's Up Movement (2018)

After the Harvey Weinstein scandal exploded into the headlines in October 2017, more women came forward to accuse dozens of other prominent men in Hollywood of sexual misconduct. These high-profile disclosures inspired millions of women around the world to share their own stories on social media using the #MeToo hashtag. The #MeToo movement proved highly effective in raising public awareness of the pervasiveness of sexual predation and creating a sense of community among survivors.

Some powerful women in the entertainment industry sought to build upon the momentum generated by #MeToo by taking action to solve the problem. They called their initiative "Time's Up," declaring that "the clock has run out on sexual assault, harassment, and inequality in the workplace. It's time to do something about it" (Time's Up 2017). The Time's Up movement aimed to promote fundamental changes in laws, policies, and workplace cultures to eliminate the power imbalances that facilitate sexual harassment. "The struggle for women to break in, to rise up the ranks, and to simply be heard and acknowledged in male-dominated workplaces must end; time's up on this impenetrable monopoly," the movement's founders declared (Buckley 2018).

Launch of a New Movement

The initial meetings for what eventually became the Time's Up organization took place in late October 2017, when a group of female talent agents got together at the offices of the Creative Artists Agency (CAA). Within a few weeks, the meetings had expanded to include more than 100 prominent women involved in film, television, and theater, including actresses, writers, directors, producers, and studio executives. Small groups met in homes and offices in Los Angeles, New York, and London to discuss ways to use their collective influence to make positive changes. Their first order of business, according to Bad Robot executive Katie McGrath, was to determine "what we wanted out of this moment, and what was going to be required in order to shift and pivot from this horror to structural change" (Buckley 2018). The Time's Up organizers wanted to move beyond reporting experiences of sexual harassment to address the underlying workplace conditions that allowed abuse to occur. "They didn't come together because they wanted to whine, or complain, or tell a story or bemoan," said Maria Eitel, cochair of the Nike Foundation and a moderator of the early meetings. "They came together because they intended to act" (Buckley 2018).

The Time's Up mission came into focus in November 2017, when organizers received a passionate letter from the Alianza Nacional de Campesinas (National Farmworker Women's Alliance), an organization representing 700,000 female agricultural workers. The letter noted that the farmworkers stood in solidarity with the celebrities who came forward with allegations of sexual misconduct against Weinstein. It also discussed the "constant threat" of sexual violence faced by working-class women, who often lacked the resources and platform to fight back. "We understand the hurt, confusion, isolation, and betrayal that you might feel," the letter read. "But, deep in our hearts we know that it is not our fault. The only people at fault are the individuals who choose to abuse their power to harass, threaten, and harm us, like they have harmed you" (Cardenas 2018).

The letter from the Campesinas made the celebrity founders of Time's Up determined to use their wealth, privilege, and media access to help working-class women, women of color, LGBTQ individuals, and other marginalized groups that had fewer resources to combat sexual violence. Toward this end, they created the Time's Up Legal Defense Fund, managed by the National Women's Law Center, to provide legal and financial support to victims of sexual harassment who could not afford it on their own. "Time's Up was founded on the premise that everyone, every human being, deserves a right to earn a living, to take care of themselves, to take care of their families, free of the impediments of harassment and sexual assault and discrimination," said CAA executive Christy Haubegger (Langone 2018).

The Time's Up organization announced the initiative by publishing a full-page letter in the *New York Times* on January 1, 2018. More than 300 well-known figures in the entertainment industry signed the letter, including America Ferrera, Rashida Jones, Ashley Judd, Alyssa Milano, Natalie Portman, Emma Stone, Meryl Streep, and Kerry Washington. "If this group of women can't fight for a model for other women who don't have as much power and privilege, then who can?" noted television producer Shonda Rhimes (Buckley 2018). Bolstered by large donations from many celebrities, the Time's Up GoFundMe campaign collected $21 million for the legal defense fund within two months (Langone 2018).

A Multifaceted Approach

The Time's Up activists created volunteer-led working groups to address several aspects of workplace discrimination affecting women, including gender inequality in pay and advancement opportunities. They viewed inequality and power imbalances in the workplace as factors that contributed to harassment behavior. "This is a symptom of a larger, systemic inequality and a systemic pattern of exclusion for women, for people of color, and a lack of equilibrium in the power distribution in our business," Haubegger explained. "If you want to solve sexual harassment, you actually needed to solve all of those things. So we decided to really focus on that aspect" (Langone 2018).

One Time's Up working group focused on lobbying for legislation and policies to promote equal pay and equal opportunity for female workers in all industries. Another group created the Commission on Sexual Harassment and Advancing Equality in the Workplace to formulate a plan to end rampant sexual harassment in media and entertainment. Led by law professor Anita Hill (1956–)—whose testimony during the 1991 Senate confirmation hearings for Supreme Court nominee Clarence Thomas (1948–) brought workplace sexual harassment to national attention—the commission planned to study successful anti-harassment programs and practices that had been implemented by various types of organizations.

Time's Up organizers created a working group called 50/50 by 2020 aimed at achieving gender parity in the leadership ranks of entertainment-related businesses. Another group advocated for legislation to punish companies that covered up or failed to address sexual harassment complaints. It specifically focused on ending the use of nondisclosure agreements, such as those signed by several Weinstein accusers as part of financial settlements, to prevent victims of sexual abuse from speaking publicly about their experiences and holding perpetrators accountable.

The final aspect of the ambitious Time's Up initiative involved a public demonstration of solidarity at the Golden Globe Awards on January 7, 2018. Organizers urged attendees to show their support for the movement by wearing black and by taking advantage of the media exposure to speak out against sexual harassment and gender inequality. The organizers chose black to emphasize the seriousness of the issue and to shift viewers' focus from attendees' outfits to their message. "This is a moment of solidarity, not a fashion moment," said actress Eva Longoria. "For years, we've sold these awards shows as women, with our gowns and colors and our beautiful faces and our glamour.... This time the industry can't expect us to go up and twirl around. That's not what this moment is about" (Buckley 2018). Supporters introduced the hashtag #WhyWeWearBlack on social media to raise awareness of the cause.

Several film stars took the initiative a step further by inviting female activists of color to attend the Golden Globes as their dates. Actress Michelle Williams (1980–)—who became a symbol of the Time's Up movement when she received the industry minimum wage of $800 for reshooting scenes for the 2017 film *All the Money in the World*, while her male costar Mark Wahlberg received $1.5 million for doing the same work—started the trend by asking #MeToo founder Tarana Burke (1973–) to accompany her. Burke suggested that Williams's gesture would make an even more powerful statement if other stars followed her lead. "I said inviting me is great, but it could be seen as a novelty to have all these people on the red carpet and then have one activist," Burke recalled. "But what would it look like to have the red carpet flooded with all these women doing kick-a** work around the country?" (Wagmeister 2018). Other actresses who arrived at the Golden Globes with activists in tow included Meryl Streep with Ai-Jen Poo, director of the National Domestic Workers Alliance, and Laura Dern with Mónica Ramírez, cofounder of the Alianza Nacional de Campesinas.

Although the Time's Up movement received widespread praise for its fundraising efforts, it came under criticism from some quarters. Actress Rose McGowan (1973–), one of the first Weinstein accusers to come forward, dismissed the blackout protest as "Hollywood fakery" and noted that she had not been invited to the Golden Globes. *New York Times* arts critic Amanda Hess also found the frequent mentions of Time's Up at the awards ceremony disingenuous, charging that the entertainment industry "has skirted a conversation about its culture of harassment in favor of one about what an amazing job it is doing combating that harassment" (Hess 2018). Other commentators, however, praised the Time's Up organizers for taking important steps in the long process of social change.

Further Reading

Buckley, Cara. 2018. "Powerful Hollywood Women Unveil Anti-Harassment Action Plan." *New York Times*, January 1. https://www.nytimes.com/2018/01/01/movies/times-up-hollywood-women-sexual-harassment.html

Cardenas, Cat. 2018. "Meet the Women of Alianza Nacional de Campesinas, the Org That Inspired Hollywood's Time's Up Initiative." *Remezcla*, January 29. http://remezcla.com/features/culture/alianza-nacional-de-campesinas -times-up/

Hess, Amanda. 2018. "Hollywood Uses the Very Women It Exploited to Change the Subject." *New York Times*, January 24. https://www.nytimes.com /2018/01/24/arts/can-hollywood-fix-its-harassment-problem-while -celebrating-itself.html

Langone, Alix. 2018. "#MeToo and Time's Up Founders Explain the Difference between the Two Movements—And How They're Alike." *Time*, March 8. http://time.com/5189945/whats-the-difference-between-the-metoo-and -times-up-movements/

Time's Up. 2017. https://www.timesupnow.com/

Wagmeister, Elizabeth. 2018. "Tarana Burke on Hollywood, Time's Up, and Me Too Backlash." *Variety*, April 10. http://variety.com/2018/biz/news/ tarana-burke-times-up-me-too-backlash-1202748822/

CHAPTER THREE

Impacts of the #MeToo Movement

This section examines the impact of the #MeToo movement on specific areas of American life and culture, from the changes it has wrought in entertainment, business, and politics to debates about the sincerity and value of apologies offered by men accused of sexual misconduct.

#MeToo in Entertainment and the Arts

The #MeToo movement got its start in the entertainment industry in October 2017 with the allegations of sexual misconduct against Hollywood film mogul Harvey Weinstein. Before long, hundreds of women, and a few men, came forward to accuse well-known actors, directors, producers, agents, and studio executives of sexual harassment or assault. The #MeToo movement revealed a toxic culture permeating the industry, in which powerful men took advantage of their influential positions to prey on young women hoping to make it in show business. Many of these men saw their reputations sullied or careers ended, while a few—such as comedian and television icon Bill Cosby—were convicted of crimes and imprisoned.

The #MeToo disclosures led to several high-profile initiatives aimed at eradicating sexual harassment from film, television, and other industries. In January 2018, more than 300 powerful women of Hollywood launched an initiative called Time's Up to promote changes in laws, policies, and workplace cultures and provide legal and financial resources to help victims hold perpetrators accountable. Time's Up activists demonstrated their solidarity by wearing black to the 2018 Golden Globe Awards. Hollywood film studios, production companies, and talent agencies responded by adopting codes of conduct for employees, providing mandatory anti-harassment training, and creating more effective reporting mechanisms, such as designating individuals on movie sets to hear complaints. *Wonder Woman 1984* (to be released in 2019) became one of the first films to put these measures into place after producer Brett Ratner was accused of sexual misconduct on the set of the first installment in the franchise.

Many companies in the film industry also revamped their employment contracts to include morals clauses, giving them the right to fire anyone accused of inappropriate behavior. After actor Kevin Spacey was accused of sexual assault, director Ridley Scott recast him in the role of J. Paul Getty in *All the Money in the World* (2017). If Spacey's contract featured a morals clause, the studio could have sued him to recover the $10 million cost of reshooting all of his scenes with Christopher Plummer replacing him in the role. Some studios also moved toward eliminating the use of nondisclosure agreements, which had been used by the Weinstein Company and other businesses to prevent victims of sexual abuse from speaking publicly about their experiences.

Time's Up supporters argued that the lack of women executives, directors, writers, and crew members created power imbalances that facilitated sexual harassment in Hollywood. According to a survey of the 100 highest-grossing films of 2017 conducted by the Center for the Study of Women in Television and Film at San Diego State University, women accounted for only 8 percent of directors, 10 percent of writers, and 24 percent of producers (Morris 2018).

In her acceptance speech at the 90th Academy Awards in March 2018, Best Actress winner Frances McDormand challenged Hollywood to address the inequity by adopting inclusion riders—contractual arrangements specifying that a certain percentage of people hired to work on a project must be women and minorities. Several prominent figures in the entertainment industry immediately announced that their production companies would use inclusion riders for future projects, including Michael B. Jordan of Outlier Society, Ben Affleck and Matt Damon of Pearl Street Films, and Paul Feig of Feigco Entertainment. Partly due to pressure from #MeToo and Time's Up activists, demand for female writers and directors showed signs of increasing in 2018. A record number of women received deals for fall 2018 broadcast TV pilots, and women directed 37 percent of the films shown at the prestigious Sundance Film Festival that year (Morris 2018).

Although many companies in the entertainment industry took steps to distance themselves from men accused of sexual misconduct, the #MeToo movement did not appear to have as much impact on the viewing choices of film and television audiences. In a survey of 2,200 adults conducted in May 2018, 47 percent indicated that they would be less likely to watch a movie or TV show starring an actor facing #MeToo allegations, while 34 percent said it would have no effect on their viewership. When asked about 20 specific actors accused of sexual misconduct, however, respondents only identified two—Kevin Spacey and Louis C.K.—whose work they would be less likely to watch. The survey results suggested that the large number of #MeToo allegations made it difficult for viewers to remember the details of individual cases, plus the public showed a strong tendency to forgive misbehavior by their favorite stars (Piacenza 2018).

#MeToo in the Music Industry

The world of popular music has long been characterized by a culture of excess—a fast-living, hard-partying atmosphere of "sex, drugs, and rock and roll." Sexual misconduct flourished in this environment, as successful artists, agents, and executives frequently abused their positions of power and influence. Stories abounded of rock stars committing statutory rape of underage female "groupies," or music executives demanding sexual favors of aspiring female recording artists, yet fans and industry insiders dismissed such behavior as an expected part of the music business. Many women felt reluctant to speak out, meanwhile, due to fear of retaliation in the highly competitive industry.

As the #MeToo movement got underway, only a few high-profile men in the music industry faced allegations of sexual misconduct, such as Russell Simmons, founder of the Def Jam hip-hop label; Antonio "L.A." Reid, head of Epic Records; and recording artist R. Kelly. "The film industry appears to have numerous monsters within, but in the music industry, the problem may be more systemic," said Alan Williams, an academic who studies the music business. "It can be harder to identify specific villains when the very act of aspiring to a musical career requires numerous small acts of compromise and acquiescence" (McDermott 2018). In addition, men accused of sexual misconduct seemed to face fewer career repercussions in the music industry. Reid, for instance, bounced back with a new record label a few months after sexual harassment allegations forced him to step down from his post at Epic Records.

The #MeToo reckoning began to reach the music industry in August 2017, when pop star Taylor Swift testified in court against a radio host she accused of groping her. Her defiant testimony set an example for other women to follow, as she refused "to retreat from a confident and combative stance as a victim of an alleged sexual assault, in an environment and a culture that typically shames, discredits, and marginalizes women—even celebrities—who take that stance" (Fallon 2017).

In January 2018, a study by the Annenberg Inclusion Initiative at the University of Southern California revealed significant gender inequity in the music business. Of the top 100 songs released each year from 2012 to 2017, it found that female artists accounted for only 22 percent, female songwriters received credit on only 12 percent, and female producers contributed to only 2 percent. In addition, women in the music industry garnered only 9 percent of all Grammy Award nominations during that time period (Roberts and Brown 2018).

In response, a group of prominent female music executives founded Voices In Entertainment to call for an end to gender discrimination and sexual harassment in the industry. Inspired by the black dresses worn by Time's Up activists at the Golden Globes, supporters wore white roses to express solidarity during the 2018 Grammy Awards. Singer Janelle Monáe discussed the movement's goals in a powerful speech during the ceremony. Afterward, singer Kesha performed her nominated song "Praying," about her efforts to overcome alleged sexual assault by producer Dr. Luke, accompanied by a group of female stars wearing white. Supporters hoped that the initiative would spark positive changes to the culture of the music industry.

#MeToo in the Fashion Industry

In the fashion industry, which has long operated on the philosophy that "sex sells," women often faced a working environment rife with sexual harassment. Models—many of them teenagers—were objectified and exploited by agents, designers, stylists, photographers, and others who held the power to make or break their careers. With the rise of the #MeToo movement, such big-name models as Kate Upton and Amber Valetta began speaking out about rampant sexual misconduct in the industry. Models told stories of being pressured to appear nude or in sexually suggestive positions, having their images shared without permission, and being touched inappropriately. Model, filmmaker, and activist Sara Ziff criticized the culture of the fashion industry for normalizing such behavior. "It's been well known for decades that sexual abuse of models is a pervasive problem," she said. "The issue is not just the individuals who've abused their power, but also the industry's enabling culture and lack of accountability, and the sense that this kind of predatory behavior just comes with the territory" (Pressler 2018).

When the #MeToo reckoning first struck the fashion industry, it took the form of dozens of male models coming forward to accuse the famous photographers Mario Testino and Bruce Weber of sexual misconduct. Several female models also resurrected longstanding sexual-abuse allegations against photographer Terry Richardson, who responded by claiming that all of the subjects of his sexually explicit works participated consensually. Hundreds more models shared stories of sexual harassment on social media.

Although some advertisers, magazines, and agencies severed their relationships with the alleged abusers, the industry as a whole came under criticism for its tepid response. In fact, some prominent insiders responded by defending the industry's practices and condemning the models who complained about mistreatment. Designer Karl Lagerfeld, for instance, derided the sexual assault allegations against Karl Templer, creative director for *Interview* magazine. "I don't believe a word of it. A girl complained he tried to pull her pants down and he is instantly excommunicated from a profession that up until then had venerated him," he stated. "It's unbelievable. If you don't want your pants pulled about, don't become a model! Join a nunnery, there'll always be a place for you in the convent" (Gardner 2018).

In an effort to improve the experience of models in the industry, the Council of Fashion Designers of America (CDFA) instituted new rules requiring designers to provide private changing areas for runway models at 2018 New York fashion week shows. Before this time, models dressed in the same backstage areas where designers and media gathered after the shows. Several designers and activists also used the platform of fashion week to draw attention to problems in the industry. For example, Myriam Chalek organized a Time's Up Show to showcase models' experiences of sexual harassment. Each model wore angel's wings and shared her story on the catwalk while chained to a man in a pig mask. Other designers incorporated #MeToo and women's rights themes into their collections, including Michelle Smith of Milly and Stacey Bendet of Alice + Olivia.

#MeToo in Art and Literature

Women in the world of art responded immediately to the #MeToo revelations in Hollywood. In October 2017, more than 2,000 artists, curators, educators, and writers spoke out against workplace sexual harassment in an open letter entitled "Not Surprised." They drew the title from a phrase in artist Jenny Holtzer's *Truisms* series, "Abuse of power comes as no surprise." "We have been groped, undermined, harassed, infantilized, scorned, threatened, and intimidated by those in positions of power who control access to resources and opportunities," they wrote. "We have held our tongues, threatened by power wielded over us and promises of institutional access and career advancement" (Frank 2017a). The letter followed accusations of sexual harassment against Knight Landesman, the former publisher of *ArtForum* magazine.

The #MeToo movement also prompted a reassessment of works of art that objectify or sexualize women, as well as works created by artists accused of mistreating women. Critics contended that museums have a responsibility to challenge the misogynistic views expressed in works such as Paul Gauguin's Polynesian paintings, which depict nude teenage girls who reportedly served as his sex slaves. Some critics argued that museums should remove questionable works from their collections. Others asserted that museums should continue to display the works but provide context, in the form of wall text or discussion programs, to help patrons understand the power imbalance between artist and subject and its implications for the subject's agency and consent.

Although most museums kept works of historical significance, some removed the works of contemporary artists accused of sexual misconduct during the #MeToo reckoning. The National Museum of Art in Washington, D.C., for instance, canceled an exhibition by the portrait artist Chuck Close after eight women claimed that he behaved inappropriately toward them. Other art institutions adapted to the #MeToo era by diversifying their programs and collections to include more women and artists of color. "We need to make space for other voices, whether historical or contemporary," said a New York art educator. "We need *other* perspectives besides a white male perspective, besides a misogynist perspective. How many voices do we need that keep reinforcing misogyny?" (Frank 2017b).

Fallout from the #MeToo movement also struck the world of literature. In February 2018, fantasy writer Anne Ursu wrote an article for *Medium* alleging rampant sexual harassment at American publishing industry conferences and book festivals. Many of the incidents she described involved prominent male authors and editors who took advantage of their positions of influence to make unwanted sexual advances toward women hoping to build literary careers. Ursu's exposé resulted in several prominent authors being dropped by their agents or publishers, including James Dashner (*The Maze Runner*), Jay Asher (*13 Reasons Why*), and Sherman Alexie (*The Absolutely True Diary of a Part-Time Indian*). Publishers responded by adopting zero-tolerance policies and inserting morality clauses in author contracts.

In May 2018, the Swedish Academy announced that it would not award the prestigious Nobel Prize in Literature for the first time since World War II due to a sexual harassment scandal involving the French photographer Jean-Claude Arnault. Eighteen women came forward to accuse Arnault of sexual misconduct in incidents that spanned two decades. Some of the women claimed that Arnault assaulted them at Nobel Prize banquets and that the Academy never responded to their complaints. Academy members determined that the allegations compromised the integrity of the award since Arnault's wife, poet Katarina Frostenson, sat on the committee that decided the winner.

Further Reading

Cartner-Morley, Jess. 2018. "New York Fashion Week: Industry Faces Its #MeToo Moment." *Guardian*, February 10. https://www.theguardian.com/fashion/2018/feb/10/new-york-fashion-week-industry-faces-metoo-moment

Fallon, Kevin. 2017. "Taylor Swift's No-Bulls**t Testimony at Groping Trial: 'He Grabbed My A**.'" *Daily Beast*, August 10. https://www.thedailybeast.com/taylor-swifts-no-bullshit-testimony-at-groping-trial-he-grabbed-my-ass

Frank, Priscilla. 2017a. "In the #MeToo Era, Do These Paintings Still Belong in a Museum?" *Huffington Post*, December 14. https://www.huffingtonpost.com/entry/museums-me-too-sexual-harassment-art_us_5a2ae382e4b0a290f0507176

Frank, Priscilla. 2017b. "2,000 Women Are Speaking Out against Rampant Sexual Harassment in the Art World." *Huffington Post*, October 30. https://www.huffingtonpost.com/entry/2000-women-are-speaking-out-against-rampant-sexual-harassment-in-the-art-world_us_59f740c0e4b077d8dfcb2d43

Gardner, Abby. 2018. "Designer Karl Lagerfeld: 'I'm Fed Up with #MeToo.'" *Glamour*, April 13. https://www.glamour.com/story/designer-karl-lagerfeld-im-fed-up-with-metoo

McDermott, Maeve. 2018. "Why #MeToo Hasn't Taken Off in the Music Industry." *USA Today*, January 22. https://www.usatoday.com/story/life/music/2018/01/22/news-views-why-metoo-hasnt-taken-off-music-industry/1028741001/

Morris, Regan. 2018. "Is #MeToo Changing Hollywood?" BBC News, March 3. https://www.bbc.com/news/world-us-canada-43219531

Piacenza, Joanna. 2018. "How #MeToo Impacts Viewers' Decisions on What to Watch." *Morning Consult*, May 28. https://morningconsult.com/2018/05/28/how-metoo-impacts-viewers-decisions-what-watch/

Pressler, Jessica, and Alexa Toulis-Reay. 2018. "Can Fashion Ever Be an Ethical Business?" *Cut*, February 6. https://www.thecut.com/2018/02/will-fashion-have-a-metoo-moment.html

Roberts, Randall, and August Brown. 2018. "Open Letter Inspired by #TimesUp Asks for White-Rose Show of Support at Grammy Awards." *Los Angeles Times*, January 25. http://www.latimes.com/entertainment/music/la-et-ms-grammy-times-up-20180125-story.html

Ursu, Anne. 2018. "Sexual Harassment in the Children's Book Industry." *Medium*, February 7, 2018. https://medium.com/@anneursu_10179/sexual-harassment-in-the-childrens-book-industry-3417048ccde2

#MeToo in American Politics

The momentum for the #MeToo movement began building during the 2016 presidential election campaign. The contest featured the first female candidate from a major political party, Democrat Hillary Clinton, which brought issues of gender equality and sexism to the forefront of American politics. Sexual harassment emerged as a topic of national discussion shortly before the November election, when the media released footage from a 2005 television appearance by Donald Trump in which the Republican candidate seemingly boasted about taking advantage of his celebrity to grope women. When Trump became president despite facing allegations of sexual misconduct, millions of women around the world expressed their determination to stand up for their rights by participating in the January 2017 Women's March. "I think Trump's victory proved to women—if you did not support him—you could draw two conclusions," said Clinton aide Jennifer Palmieri. "Women were only meant to go so far, and men like that were meant to win in America, or we were playing by an outdated set of rules that women politicians and women in business followed for decades" (Nilsen 2018).

Sexual harassment was a pervasive problem in American politics long before the 2016 presidential race, however. Powerful men dominate the political sphere, and many have abused their influence over female employees to demand sexual favors or make unwanted advances. Since politicians operate in an intense media spotlight, some of the most highly publicized allegations of sexual harassment have centered around political figures. The 1991 Senate confirmation hearings for Supreme Court nominee Clarence Thomas, for instance, launched a national debate about the treatment of women in the workplace when former employee Anita Hill claimed in televised testimony that Thomas had sexually harassed her. President Bill Clinton also became embroiled in scandal over allegations of sexual misconduct and faced impeachment over his affair with a White House intern.

The rise of the #MeToo movement in the fall of 2017 produced a flurry of allegations against prominent figures in the federal government. Several women came forward in November to accuse Roy Moore, a Republican Senate candidate from Alabama, of making sexual advances toward them when they were teenagers. Although Moore continued to garner support from Trump, the allegations contributed to his defeat in the special election to replace Jeff Sessions, who left his seat in Congress to serve as Trump's attorney general. A week after the Moore allegations came to light, radio host Leeann Tweeden accused Senator Al Franken, a Democrat from Minnesota, of groping her during a USO tour in 2006. Franken apologized for behaving inappropriately and resigned from office. In December, Democrat John Conyers of Michigan stepped down from his seat in the U.S. House of Representatives after being accused of making unwanted sexual advances toward staff members. Sexual harassment allegations also prompted the resignations of Republican representatives Trent Franks of Arizona, Blake Farenthold of Texas, and Pat Meehan of Pennsylvania, as well as federal judge Alex Kozinski of the Ninth Circuit U.S. Court of Appeals.

The #MeToo movement also revealed patterns of inappropriate behavior in state legislatures. Two weeks after the Harvey Weinstein scandal rocked Hollywood, the *Los Angeles Times* published an open letter signed by nearly 150 female legislators, staff members, political consultants, and lobbyists expressing concerns about rampant sexual harassment and gender discrimination in the California state government. Another letter described similar concerns about the atmosphere in Illinois state politics. Oregon state senator Sara Gelser made headlines in November by accusing fellow senator Jeff Kruse of subjecting her to inappropriate touching for years, despite her repeated complaints to the legislature's human resources and legal departments. Allegations of sexual misconduct eventually encompassed at least 40 lawmakers from 20 states (Ebert 2017).

A Partisan Divide in #MeToo Responses

In the political realm, the response to sexual misconduct allegations against public officials tended to be governed by party allegiance. When Anita Hill testified before the Senate Judiciary Committee in 1991, for instance, Republican members attacked her credibility, questioned her motivations for coming forward, and disputed her account of events in an effort to secure Thomas's confirmation. Similarly, many feminists stood behind Democrat Bill Clinton—whom they viewed as a valuable ally in the fight for women's rights—and vilified the women who accused him of sexual misconduct. The pattern continued during the #MeToo era, when most Republican voters either dismissed the allegations against Trump as untrue or decided that his conduct did not disqualify him from serving as president.

Although people on both sides of the partisan divide were more likely to overlook #MeToo allegations against members of their own party, polls showed significant differences between Democrats and Republicans. A survey of 2,350 adults conducted by *Time* magazine in November 2017 found that 74 percent of Democrats agreed that a Democratic congressman accused of sexual harassment should resign from office, while only 54 percent of Republicans said that a Republican congressman should resign over such allegations (Alter 2017). In his resignation speech, Franken alluded to what he viewed as inconsistent standards being applied to Trump and Moore. "There is some irony in the fact that I am leaving," he stated, "while a man who has bragged on tape about his history of sexual assault sits in the Oval Office, and a man who has repeatedly preyed on young girls campaigns for the Senate with the full support of his party" (Franken 2017).

The Impact of #MeToo on Government

The #MeToo movement raised awareness of gender inequity in all levels of government. Women held less than 20 percent of seats in the U.S. Congress as of 2017, for instance, and less than 25 percent of seats in state legislatures nationwide. Some #MeToo supporters argued that increasing the number of women in office would help eliminate the power imbalances that facilitated sexual harassment. The sense of empowerment generated by the movement contributed to a record 309 female candidates running for seats in the House of Representatives as of April 2018, along with a record 40 women running for governor in various states. In addition, the pro-choice political action organization Emily's List reported that it received 34,000 inquiries from women interested in running for office in 2018, compared to 920 in 2016 (Nilsen 2018).

Political leaders responded to #MeToo by putting new rules in place to prevent sexual harassment and hold perpetrators accountable. The U.S. Congress, for instance, required all officeholders and staff members to attend mandatory anti-harassment training. "Sexual harassment really is abuse of power," said Merrick Rossein, an attorney who helped the New York Assembly overhaul its sexual harassment policies. "You have powerful people, so you have to know it's likely to happen. So, knowing it's likely to happen, what would a prudent, reasonable person or institution do to prevent it or to stop it when it occurs?" (Vock 2017).

#MeToo encouraged many state legislatures and local governments to review and revise their sexual harassment policies and training programs as well. In Illinois, state legislators established a watchdog position to oversee the handling of harassment complaints and appointed a former federal prosecutor to fill it. Arizona lawmakers proposed legislation banning the use of nondisclosure agreements to silence victims in sexual harassment cases and voiding those already in effect. The Maryland General Assembly reformed its policies to require appointment of an independent investigator to handle sexual harassment complaints and to prohibit lawmakers from using taxpayer funds to pay settlements.

#MeToo Prompts a Reassessment of Old Charges

Seeing men's political careers collapse under the fallout of the #MeToo reckoning prompted some observers to reassess the legacies of powerful men who faced sexual misconduct charges in earlier eras, including Thomas and Clinton. #MeToo supporters argued that the revelations forced people to recognize the devastating impact of sexual harassment and the importance of holding men accountable. In this environment, a woman came forward with new allegations about Thomas in 2017, claiming that he groped her at a dinner party in 1999. Her allegations prompted journalists to investigate the story behind his controversial confirmation hearings, and they found several witnesses to corroborate Hill's testimony that Thomas discussed pornographic films at work. Since Thomas denied those charges under oath during his confirmation hearings, critics argued that he had committed perjury and called for his impeachment from the Supreme Court.

Feminists pointed out that Thomas's confirmation had far-reaching implications for women's rights, which he consistently voted to restrict throughout his quarter-century of service on the court. "His worldview, with its consistent objectification of women, is the one that's shaping the contours of what's possible for women in America today, more than that of just about any man alive, save for his fellow justices," wrote Jill Abramson (2018). Thomas voted against reproductive rights, insurance coverage for contraception, and equal-pay protections. He also voted with the narrow majority in Vance v. Ball State University (2013) to limit employer liability in workplace sexual harassment cases by narrowing the definition of "supervisor." The #MeToo movement also prompted Joe Biden, who served as chairman of the Senate Judiciary Committee during Thomas's confirmation hearings and as vice president under President Barack Obama, to apologize to Hill for not doing more to support her.

The #MeToo movement also caused some Democrats to reconsider their earlier support for President Bill Clinton in light of the sexual misconduct complaints made against him by four women in incidents that allegedly occurred between 1978 and 1993. Several liberal journalists wrote articles arguing that Clinton should have resigned from office over the allegations, and Democratic Senator Kirsten Gillibrand publicly agreed with their assessment. Other critics claimed that Clinton's affair with White House intern Monica Lewinsky, which they both described as consensual at the time, constituted sexual misconduct given the enormous power imbalance between the two parties.

When asked whether the #MeToo movement forced him to rethink his past behavior, however, Clinton defended his political legacy and pointed to his record of supporting women's issues throughout his career in public service. Critics argued that Clinton's justifications no longer excused his behavior in the #MeToo era. They also claimed that Democrats' defense of him during the 1990s delayed the national conversation about sexual harassment for decades, allowing other powerful men to abuse women with impunity. "The widespread liberal response to the sex-crime accusations against Bill Clinton found their natural consequence 20 years later in the behavior of Harvey Weinstein: Stay loudly and publicly and extravagantly on the side of signal leftist causes and you can do what you want in the privacy of your offices and hotel rooms," wrote Caitlin Flanagan. "But the mood of the country has changed. We are in a time when old monuments are coming down and men are losing their careers over things they did to women a long time ago" (Flanagan 2017).

Further Reading

Abramson, Jill. 2018. "Do You Believe Her Now?" *New York Magazine*, February 18. http://nymag.com/daily/intelligencer/2018/02/the-case-for-impeaching -clarence-thomas.html

Alter, Charlotte, 2017. "Republicans Are Less Likely Than Democrats to Believe Women Who Make Sexual Assault Accusations." *Time*, December 6. http://time.com/5049665/republicans-democrats-believe-sexual-assault -accusations-survey/

Ebert, Joel. 2017. "Sexual Harassment Troubles Mount in Statehouses around the Country." *USA Today*, November 20. https://www.usatoday.com/story/ news/nation-now/2017/11/20/sexual-harassment-statehouses/882874001/

Flanagan, Caitlin. 2017. "Bill Clinton: A Reckoning." *Atlantic*, November 13. https://www.theatlantic.com/entertainment/archive/2017/11/reckoning -with-bill-clintons-sex-crimes/545729/

Franken, Al. 2017. "Al Franken's Resignation Speech." CNN, December 7. https:// www.cnn.com/2017/12/07/politics/speech-al-franken-transcript/index.html

Nilsen, Ella. 2018. "A Record-Setting Number of Women Are Running for the House in 2018." *Vox*, April 6. https://www.vox.com/policy-and-politics/ 2018/4/6/17205790/women-running-congress-house-2018-record

Vock, Daniel C. 2017. "As Outcry over Sexual Harassment Grows, Focus Shifts to State Legislatures." *Governing*, October 18. http://www.governing.com/ topics/politics/gov-sexual-harassment-state-legislatures.html

#MeToo and the News Media

The news media played a complicated role in the #MeToo movement. Investigative journalists Jodi Kantor and Megan Twohey helped launch the movement in October 2017 by revealing the extensive sexual misconduct allegations against Hollywood producer Harvey Weinstein in a *New York Times* exposé. Other reporters uncovered and publicized sexual harassment scandals involving prominent figures in academia, business, entertainment, and politics. The work of these journalists raised public awareness of the #MeToo movement and increased its cultural impact. In addition to these contributions, however, the news media became implicated in the #MeToo reckoning when several prominent journalists joined the ranks of accused perpetrators.

Like many other industries, the news media predominantly features men in positions of power. Young, inexperienced reporters often depend on these men for assignments, guidance, and career advancement. Such power imbalances create a workplace environment where sexual harassment is more likely to occur. The *Columbia Journalism Review* found that 41 percent of staff journalists and 47 percent of freelancers experienced sexual harassment in the newsroom. Two-thirds did not report the sexual harassment, however, due to fear of career repercussions (Edge 2018).

The problem of sexual harassment in the news media came to light even before the #MeToo movement got underway. In July 2016, Fox News chairman Roger Ailes resigned after several employees, including news anchors Gretchen Carlson and Megyn Kelly, lodged complaints against him. In April 2017, the *New York Times* revealed that Fox News had paid millions of dollars in settlements to six women who accused news program host Bill O'Reilly of sexual misconduct. Although O'Reilly disputed the charges, Fox fired him after his program lost more than half of its advertisers.

Once the outpouring of #MeToo disclosures began, sexual misconduct allegations surfaced in various media outlets, including radio, television, newspapers, magazines, and online platforms. The accusations targeted executives, editors, reporters, anchors, and hosts. Among the most prominent media figures to face sexual misconduct allegations were news anchor Charlie Rose, *New Republic* editor Leon Wieseltier, National Public Radio executive Michael Oreskes, CNN analyst Ryan Lizza, and *Vox* editor Lockhart Steele. Journalist Moira Donegan drew attention to the pervasiveness of sexual harassment in the industry by circulating a crowdsourced document known as the "S***ty Media Men" list, which detailed allegations against more than 70 men.

Combating Gender Bias in Media Coverage

The revelations of widespread sexual misconduct in the media industry raised questions about the extent to which sexist attitudes held by prominent figures impacted news coverage of the #MeToo movement. Critics pointed out that many of the men accused of mistreating women played a role in shaping public perceptions of sexual harassment. "The media is breaking the news here; the media is also deeply implicated in this news and still shaping how the tale is getting told," wrote journalist Rebecca Traister. "Ours is an industry, like so many others, dominated by white men at the top; they have made the decisions about what to cover and how, and they still do. The pervasiveness of these power imbalances and the way they affect how even this story itself is being told are instructive" (Traister 2017).

Critics pointed out that several high-profile media personalities who provided extensive coverage of the 2016 presidential campaign were later accused of sexual harassment, including Mark Halperin of ABC News, Matt Lauer of NBC News, and Glenn Thrush of *Politico*. *New York Times* columnist Jill Filipovic claimed that these men's sexist attitudes and actions colored their perceptions of the candidates, leading them to portray Trump more positively and Clinton more negatively. "A pervasive theme of all of these men's coverage of Mrs. Clinton was that she was dishonest and unlikable," she wrote. "These recent harassment allegations suggest that perhaps the problem wasn't that Mrs. Clinton was untruthful or inherently hard to connect with, but that these particular men hold deep biases against women who seek power instead of sticking to acquiescent sex-object status" (Filipovic 2017).

The sexual harassment scandals facing high-profile individuals damaged the overall credibility of the news media. In an effort to restore the public trust, the industry took a hard-line approach in investigating allegations and holding perpetrators accountable. Many media outlets reexamined their newsroom cultures and took steps to increase the diversity of voices shaping coverage by elevating more women to positions of power. Media leaders also held several industry-wide events aimed at developing systemic changes to end sexual harassment, such as the Power Shift Summit at the Newseum in Washington, D.C. Many industry leaders also took part in the Commission on Sexual Harassment and Advancing Equality in the Workplace, an initiative that grew out of the Time's Up movement and featured Anita Hill as chairperson.

Given the power of media to inform audiences and shape their perceptions of issues, some outlets responded to #MeToo by adjusting their subject matter to better reflect the new era. Some men's magazines, for instance, shifted away from articles focusing on topics that increasingly reflected an outdated, stereotypical concept of masculinity—such as fast cars, fast women, and a hard-partying lifestyle. Instead, they began featuring articles designed to appeal to men with more evolved, modern sensibilities and interests, such as politics, films, music, nutrition, fitness, relationships, and fatherhood.

Further Reading

Edge, Abigail. 2018. "How Newsroom Culture Is Being Reevaluated Following #MeToo." *Quill*, March 19. https://quill.spjnetwork.org/2018/03/19/ me-too-movement-journalism-matt-lauer-glenn-thrush-sexual-misconduct -media-news/

Filipovic, Jill. 2017. "The Men Who Cost Clinton the Election." *New York Times*, December 1. https://www.nytimes.com/2017/12/01/opinion/matt-lauer -hillary-clinton.html

Traister, Rebecca. 2017. "Our National Narratives Are Still Being Shaped by Lecherous, Powerful Men." *Cut*, October 27. www.thecut.com/2017/10/ halperin-wieseltier-weinstein-powerful-lecherous-men.html

Businesses Adapt to the #MeToo Era

Most of the laws prohibiting sexual harassment, such as Title VII of the Civil Rights Act, pertain to inappropriate or offensive behavior in the workplace. Sexual harassment occurs frequently in the world of business because the hierarchical reporting relationships found in most companies create power imbalances between managers and employees. Some bosses abuse their power by making unwanted sexual advances, demanding sexual favors, or creating a hostile work environment for their subordinates. Many employees feel powerless to stop or report such behavior when doing so might pose a threat to their career opportunities and economic welfare.

The rise of the #MeToo movement in the fall of 2017 revealed the pervasiveness of sexual misconduct in entertainment, media, politics, academia, and business. An ABC News/*Washington Post* poll found that 30 percent of women had experienced unwanted sexual advances at work, while an NPR/PBS NewsHour/Marist survey put the number at 35 percent (McGregor 2017). The outpouring of #MeToo disclosures empowered employees in many industries—from migrant farmworkers and hotel housekeeping staff to Wall Street financial executives and Silicon Valley software engineers—to come forward with sexual harassment complaints. As a result of these allegations, dozens of high-profile business leaders faced career repercussions, including Uber cofounder Travis Kalanick, union leaders Caleb Jennings and Scott Courtney, sports executive Terdema Ussery, and venture capitalists Shervin Pishevar, Dave McClure, and Justin Caldbeck.

Employers Face New Legal and Ethical Responsibilities

In the #MeToo era, companies faced added pressure to investigate sexual misconduct allegations fully and hold perpetrators accountable. Companies that ignored the problem came under criticism from #MeToo supporters and exposed themselves to negative publicity, legal liability, and financial costs. "Every company and organization is going to have to change now," leadership expert Gloria Feldt wrote in *Time*. "Leaders can make that change happen intentionally in ways that add value to their companies, or it will be imposed upon them by external forces and perhaps not in a way that's positive for their businesses" (Feldt 2018).

#MeToo supporters argued that businesses stood to benefit by eliminating sexual harassment. In addition to causing psychological harm to employees, they pointed out, workplace sexual harassment cost companies money both directly, through damage awards and legal fees, and indirectly, through lower productivity, higher turnover, and a disengaged workforce. In many firms, #MeToo prompted upper management to treat sexual harassment as a serious business risk, along the same lines as security or hacking. Many companies responded to the risk by strengthening their anti-harassment policies and training programs. The Equal Employment Opportunity Commission (EEOC) reported a fourfold increase in usage of the educational resources on its website in the months after the Harvey Weinstein scandal launched the #MeToo movement (Natour 2018).

In the past, many companies used training programs that focused on the legal definition of sexual harassment and specified workplace behaviors to avoid. Many companies administered these programs only to new employees through online modules that they completed individually. Coupled with anti-harassment policies listed in an employee handbook, these programs were mainly intended to insulate companies from liability in harassment lawsuits. Research suggested that such training did little to prevent workplace sexual harassment, partly because the problem did not stem from a lack of knowledge. "Do you really think that educated grown men need to be taught not to grope their co-workers?" said psychologist Louise Fitzgerald. "The fact that people don't know, well, that is nonsense" (Natour 2018).

In the wake of the #MeToo disclosures, such companies as Uber, Fox News, and NBC revamped their anti-harassment training programs to include in-person, small-group discussion sessions, which they held on a regular basis and made mandatory for all employees. Instead of focusing on prohibited behavior, the sessions aimed to build a corporate culture that valued fairness, diversity, respect, and civility. Some programs included bystander intervention training, which provided coworkers with productive tools to use when they witnessed inappropriate or offensive workplace conduct. Many companies also worked to improve their reporting procedures to make it easier for employees to come forward with complaints without fear of retaliation. For instance, some businesses introduced mobile apps or online platforms to facilitate anonymous reporting of sexual harassment or gender discrimination in the workplace.

Critics questioned whether these measures did enough to create safe work environments where employees felt empowered to report harassment. "We believe effective training can reduce workplace harassment," wrote the authors of an EEOC assessment. "However, even effective training cannot occur in a vacuum—it must be part of a holistic culture of non-harassment that starts at the top" (Feldblum and Lipnic 2016). To achieve meaningful, systemic change, critics argued that companies and their leaders—especially men—needed to publicly support the broader goals of the #MeToo movement, such as eliminating the use of nondisclosure agreements, forced arbitration, and confidential settlements. Critics charged that these legal maneuvers silenced victims of workplace harassment in the interest of protecting the company's reputation. In December 2017, Microsoft garnered praise from #MeToo activists by announcing that it would no longer require its employees to submit to confidential arbitration.

Women Face Challenges in the Workplace

In addition to drawing public attention to sexual misconduct in the workplace, the #MeToo movement highlighted persistent inequities in pay, positions, and promotion opportunities for working women. Some activists argued that the basic workplace dynamic that allowed women to be objectified, disrespected, and harassed would only change when more women attained positions of power in the business world. "It's possible that we're missing the bigger picture altogether: that this is not, at its heart, about sex at all," wrote journalist Rebecca Traister. "What it's really about is work, and women's equality in the workplace, and more broadly, about the rot at the core of our power structures that makes it harder for women to do work because the whole thing is tipped toward men" (McGregor 2017).

To support their position, activists pointed to studies showing that companies with higher percentages of women in upper management earned more money, made decisions more effectively, and responded better to competitive pressure. Since women are responsible for 70–80 percent of consumer purchasing decisions, they argued that increasing the number of women in leadership roles could also help companies understand and react to changing markets (Feldt 2018). Equal pay for equal work was another major priority of women's rights advocates, who noted that female employees typically received 80 cents for every dollar paid to male employees. One survey of human resources executives found that nearly half of companies planned to adjust their pay policies to achieve greater wage parity for male and female employees. Analysts attributed this trend to social pressure resulting from the #MeToo and Time's Up movements (Carpenter 2018). In March 2018, Starbucks announced that it had achieved the goal of 100 percent gender pay equity for its U.S. employees.

Critics, on the other hand, argued that #MeToo had a negative impact on businesses by destroying the professional camaraderie between men and women in the workplace. They claimed that the heightened awareness of sexual harassment encouraged women to view men's behavior as suspicious and predatory, creating an unproductive atmosphere of fear, distrust, and division. Many male employees expressed concern about facing harassment allegations on the basis of behavior they considered friendly and harmless, such as celebrating an accomplishment with a hug.

Researchers found evidence to support the idea that the #MeToo era produced a chilling effect on workplace relations. The effect was particularly pronounced in mentoring relationships between men in senior management and women in junior positions. A February 2018 survey conducted by the Lean In initiative found that the percentage of male executives who felt uncomfortable about mentoring female colleagues had tripled since before the Weinstein scandal. In another survey, nearly two-thirds of male managers acknowledged limiting their one-on-one interactions with female employees to avoid rumors, misunderstandings, or false allegations (Thomson 2018). "It's an incredibly dangerous message that women are almost black widow spiders waiting to catch their prey and a man should not be alone with a woman unless he has a guardian to protect him," said employment lawyer Jonathan Segal (Natour 2018).

#MeToo supporters noted that such attitudes had the effect of segregating employees by gender, which amounted to gender discrimination. They argued that the loss of mentoring opportunities had the potential to set back women's career advancement. To preserve access to mentors for female employees, experts suggested that companies formalize mentoring relationships and designate spaces for mentors to meet protégés for lunch or coffee. In the end, according to Harvard Business School professor Robin Ely, the task of breaking patterns of behavior and changing corporate cultures falls to business leaders. "It's not something you can legislate with policy," she said. "It's something that leaders need to take up as their own agenda, to really be invested in understanding how people experience the culture of the organization, a culture that they, as leaders, are responsible for, whether they like it or not" (Pazzanese and Walsh 2017).

Further Reading

Carpenter, Julia. 2018. "#MeToo and #TimesUp Have Pushed 48% of Companies to Review Pay Policies." CNN, January 28. http://money.cnn.com/2018/02/28/pf/gender-pay-gap/index.html

Feldblum, Chai R., and Victoria A. Lipnic. 2016. "Select Task Force on the Study of Harassment in the Workplace Report." *Equal Employment Opportunity Commission*, June. https://www.eeoc.gov/eeoc/task_force/harassment/report_summary.cfm

Feldt, Gloria. 2018. "How Companies Must Adapt in the #MeToo Era." *Time*, January 28. http://time.com/5120607/companies-leadership-metoo-era/

McGregor, Jena. 2017. "Another Day at Work for Many Women." *Washington Post*, December 14. https://www.washingtonpost.com/news/on-leadership/wp/2017/12/14/another-day-at-work-for-many-women-lower-pay-passed-over-treated-as-incompetent-and-subjected-to-slights/?utm_term=.6e4a991cfa0b

Natour, Rhana. 2018. "Does Sexual Harassment Training Work?" *PBS NewsHour*, January 8. https://www.pbs.org/newshour/nation/does-sexual-harassment-training-work

Pazzanese, Christina, and Colleen Walsh. 2017. "The Women's Revolt: Why Now, and Where To?" *Harvard Gazette*, December 21. https://news.harvard.edu/gazette/story/2017/12/metoo-surge-could-change-society-in-pivotal-ways-harvard-analysts-say/

Thomson, Stéphanie. 2018. "#MeToo Is Having Unexpected Consequences for Working Women." *World Economic Forum*, March 7. https://www.weforum.org/agenda/2018/03/metoo-campaign-women-isolated-at-work/

The Global Reach of #MeToo

The viral response to Alyssa Milano's #MeToo tweet extended far beyond the confines of the United States. On October 15, 2017—10 days after a parade of female celebrities began coming forward to accuse Hollywood producer Harvey Weinstein of sexual misconduct—the actress and activist asked her Twitter followers to reply "Me Too" if they had ever experienced sexual harassment or assault. By early November, Twitter data indicated that the hashtag had appeared in 2.3 million tweets that originated from 85 different countries (Fox and Diehm 2017). Social media users around the world quickly adapted the phrase to fit their own languages and cultures. Some of the trending hashtags included #YoTambien ("I as well") in Spanish, #BalanceTonPorc ("expose your pig") in French, and #quellavoltache ("that time when") in Italian. In China, where social media usage is subject to censorship, some inventive people posted responses using the hashtag #RiceBunny, which sounds like "Me Too" in Chinese.

As the #MeToo movement spread, it created a global community of women who felt empowered to share their personal accounts of enduring catcalls, lewd gestures, propositions, pinching, groping, coercion, sexual abuse, or rape. The outpouring of stories made it clear that sexual harassment and assault were pervasive problems worldwide. In Egypt, for instance, surveys showed that 99 percent of women experienced some form of sexual harassment. The situation was almost as bad for women in Brazil, where 86 percent reported experiencing unwanted sexual comments or advances in public (Senthillingham 2017). Men's attitudes about power, control, and entitlement played a role in the prevalence of sexual harassment in various countries. In Egypt, 62 percent of men found it acceptable for employers to expect sexual favors as a job requirement. In the United Kingdom, 36 percent of men between the ages of 25 and 34 found it acceptable to pinch a female coworker's rear end (Nunn 2018).

International #MeToo Movements

Although the #MeToo movement had its greatest impact in the United States, it generated significant public attention and precipitated legal and social changes in other countries, as well. In Great Britain, for example, investigative journalists with the *Financial Times* revealed that prominent business executives routinely harassed and groped the female servers at an annual men's charity gala, which convinced organizers to cancel the event. In addition, #MeToo activists circulated an anonymous, crowdsourced spreadsheet known as the Westminster Dossier that contained allegations of sexual misconduct against dozens of government ministers and members of Parliament. Although critics questioned the methods used to produce the document, the accusations of sexual harassment prompted the resignation of Defense Secretary Michael Fallon. A similar situation arose in India when Raya Sarkar, a law student at the University of California–Davis, collected a "cautionary list" of alleged sexual predators in Indian academia. Critics argued that the anonymous charges unfairly ruined men's reputations and careers without giving them an opportunity to defend themselves. Sarkar claimed that she merely elevated the voices of victims within a system that protected perpetrators.

In France, the #MeToo movement prompted government officials to propose new legislation on sexual harassment. One bill under consideration would impose fines on men who engaged in catcalling. The measures generated tremendous controversy in France, where some women considered vigorous and vocal romantic pursuits by men to be culturally acceptable. In January 2018, nearly 100 prominent French women—including the actress Catherine Deneuve—signed a letter in *Le Monde* denouncing #MeToo supporters as "puritanical" and charging that they equated "an awkward attempt to pick someone up" with sexual assault (Safronova 2018). The signers claimed that the movement portrayed women as helpless victims who were incapable of advocating for their own rights and interests. The letter generated an outpouring of condemnation on social media, with critics arguing that the signers trivialized sexual violence.

The #MeToo movement took hold in Australia when investigative journalist Tracey Spicer invited her followers on social media to discuss their experiences with sexual harassment in the media industry. Nearly 1,000 women responded, revealing the pervasiveness of the problem in Australian culture. "Globalization, connectivity, and the women's rights movement have created the perfect storm," Spicer stated. "Suddenly, we realize we're not alone. And our experiences are being believed. For the first time, men are understanding what women have suffered for centuries" (Crary 2018). Dozens of women—including Olympic medal-winning Australian swimmer Susie O'Neill—came forward to accuse television personality Don Burke, the host of a popular gardening program, of sexual misconduct spanning two decades. Although Burke denied the charges, the scandal launched a national conversation about sexual harassment that many people viewed as long overdue. "Senior federal politicians, board members, and executives are calling with ideas about how we change the culture," Spicer noted. "This investigation—and its consequences—will continue for many years to come" (Overington 2017).

Journalist Shiori Ito launched the #MeToo reckoning in Japan when she publicly accused a well-known television correspondent, Noriyuki Yamaguchi, of rape—a topic that was never discussed in Japanese society. "My coming forward made national news and shocked the public," she wrote in *Politico*. "The backlash hit me hard. I was vilified on social media and received hate messages and emails and calls from unknown numbers" (Ito 2018). Although Yamaguchi denied the charges, Ito's disclosure prompted many other women to come forward. The public attention surrounding the allegations contributed to some changes in Japanese law, including the introduction of measures broadening the definition of rape and increasing minimum sentences for sex crimes.

The impact of the #MeToo social media campaign was blunted in China, where censors reacted strongly to restrict citizens' participation in "foreign" movements or any discussion of sexual assault. Following the Weinstein scandal, however, U.S.-based academic Luo Xixi came forward to accuse a renowned Chinese professor of sexual misconduct. When students in China added their own allegations, university officials fired the professor in question and launched investigations into the behavior of several other academics. Although the incident raised public awareness of the problem of sexual harassment, #MeToo supporters questioned whether Chinese women could sustain the momentum in the face of government resistance.

Amplifying the Voices of Working Women

Activists involved in international humanitarian and women's rights issues sought to extend the #MeToo movement's global reach to include low-wage workers in developing countries. They asserted that poverty and inequality made women more vulnerable to sexual violence, yet less likely to have access to resources and support to combat it. While the #MeToo social media campaign helped improve working conditions for celebrities in Hollywood, some observers questioned whether it had any impact on the lives of ordinary women working in fields, factories, and hotels around the world.

To address this situation, some prominent activists called on the International Labor Organization (ILO) to pass a global convention defining and prohibiting workplace sexual harassment and violence. They claimed that an ILO convention would provide an important tool to help spread the impact of the #MeToo movement to more women. "It's about solidarity across all kinds of boundaries—rich or poor, black or white, North or South," said international development expert Anne Marie Goetz. "If you get an explosion of #MeToo, you start getting the protection of numbers, and a growing mass of evidence that there's a real problem—not just one individual making this up" (Crary 2018).

Further Reading

Burke, Louise. 2018. "The #MeToo Shockwave: How the Movement Has Reverberated around the World." *Telegraph*, March 9. https://www.telegraph.co.uk/news/world/metoo-shockwave/

Crary, David. 2018. "#MeToo's Global Impact: Big in Some Places, Scant in Others." NBC San Diego, March 6. https://www.nbcsandiego.com/news/national-international/Me-Too-Movement-Global-Impact-475978753.html

Fox, Kara, and Jan Diehm. 2017. "#MeToo's Global Moment: Anatomy of a Viral Campaign." CNN, November 9. https://www.cnn.com/2017/11/09/world/metoo-hashtag-global-movement/index.html

Ito, Shiori. 2018. "Saying #MeToo in Japan." *Politico*, January 2. https://www.politico.eu/article/metoo-sexual-assault-women-rights-japan/

Nunn, Michelle. 2018. "How to Make #MeToo a Truly Global Movement." *Time*, March 9. http://time.com/5192406/metoo-international-womens-day-care/

Overington, Caroline. 2017. "From Weinstein to Don Burke, the Reckoning Is Overdue." *Australian*, December 2. https://www.theaustralian.com.au/news/inquirer/from-weinstein-to-don-burke-the-reckoning-is-overdue/news-story/ae594dbc7f6c203b683de86ab17f352a

Safronova, Valeriya. 2018. "Catherine Deneuve and Others Denounce the #MeToo Movement." *New York Times*, January 9. https://www.nytimes.com/2018/01/09/movies/catherine-deneuve-and-others-denounce-the-metoo-movement.html

Senthillingham, Meera. 2017. "Sexual Harassment: How It Stands around the Globe." CNN, November 29. https://www.cnn.com/2017/11/25/health/sexual-harassment-violence-abuse-global-levels/index.html

Dating and Relationships in a #MeToo World

The initial outpouring of #MeToo stories focused mainly on sexual harassment perpetrated by powerful men in workplace settings. The movement began in October 2017, when dozens of celebrities came forward to accuse Hollywood producer Harvey Weinstein of sexual misconduct, and expanded over the next few months to ensnare prominent figures in the worlds of business, technology, politics, media, and academia. By early 2018, however, the focus of the #MeToo conversation shifted to include appropriate behavior in the context of dating and relationships. As the flood of revelations raised awareness of the pervasiveness of sexual misconduct and its traumatic impact on women's lives, many men began to reexamine their attitudes, expectations, and behavior in romantic and sexual encounters.

Aziz Ansari Allegations Shift the Conversation

Controversial allegations against comedian Aziz Ansari—known as an outspoken supporter of the #MeToo movement—served as the impetus for a public debate about coercion and consent in dating relationships. A woman using the fictitious name Grace told the feminist website *Babe* about a September 2017 date with Ansari that she described as "by far the worst experience with a man I've ever had." Grace stated she and Ansari went out to dinner and then back to his apartment, where they engaged in sexual activity. Grace claimed that Ansari repeatedly pressured her for sex, even though she felt uncomfortable and did not welcome his advances. By the time she left the apartment, Grace felt shaken and violated, and she texted Ansari the next day to tell him so. "Last night might've been fun for you, but it wasn't for me," she stated. "You ignored clear non-verbal cues; you kept going with advances. You had to have noticed I was uncomfortable.… I want to make sure you're aware so maybe the next girl doesn't have to cry on the ride home" (Way 2018).

Grace decided to tell her story in January 2018, after Ansari appeared at the Golden Globe Awards wearing a Time's Up pin, which she considered hypocritical and "cringeworthy." Ansari responded to her allegations by issuing a public statement expressing his view that their sexual encounter "by all indications was completely consensual." Ansari acknowledged that Grace had texted him the next day to say, "although 'it may have seemed okay,' upon further reflection, she felt uncomfortable," and that he responded to her message by apologizing. "It was true that everything did seem okay to me, so when I heard that it was not the case for her, I was surprised and concerned," he stated. "I took her words to heart." Ansari concluded his statement by expressing his continued support for the #MeToo movement, which he called "necessary and long overdue" (Way 2018).

The *Babe* article went viral online—attracting 2.5 million views within a week—and generated an outpouring of commentary on social media. Many women recognized Ansari's alleged predatory behavior as all too common among the men they dated. Opinions varied, however, about whether the encounter Grace described constituted sexual assault or merely a bad date. Critics charged that Grace could have expressed her objections verbally or simply left Ansari's apartment if she found his advances too aggressive or persistent. They pointed out that Ansari held no power over Grace's career, so his actions did not fit into the same category as the abuses perpetrated by Weinstein and others exposed by #MeToo. *New York Times* writer Bari Weiss found Ansari's alleged actions to be selfish, entitled, and obnoxious but asserted that Ansari did not deserve to have his reputation and career ruined for the crime of "not being a mind reader." Weiss warned that the *Babe* article could also damage the campaign against sexual misconduct, calling it "arguably the worst thing that has happened to the #MeToo movement since it began in October. It transforms what ought to be a movement for women's empowerment into an emblem for female helplessness" (Weiss 2018).

Some #MeToo supporters, on the other hand, argued that if Ansari failed to respect Grace's boundaries, then his conduct qualified as sexual assault. They asserted that he had a responsibility to check for consent at multiple points during their sexual encounter, and that he should have stopped in the absence of a positive response indicating her free and enthusiastic agreement to participate. Even if society considered pressure, coercion, and manipulation to be commonplace, stereotypical masculine behavior, supporters said the #MeToo movement clearly demonstrated that such actions did not necessarily lead to positive sexual experiences for women. "It is the sheer commonness of Grace's experience that makes it so important to talk about," Caroline Framke wrote in *Vox*. "What else is this reckoning for, if not to break down the norms that let sexual coercion flourish in the first place?" (Framke 2018).

Impact of #MeToo on the Dating Scene

The disclosures of the #MeToo movement created an opportunity for people to engage in broader discussions about acceptable conduct in romantic relationships. In a January 2018 MTV survey of 1,800 single men and women between the ages of 18 and 25, 85 percent of respondents said that the #MeToo campaign had started an important conversation about sexual harassment and assault, while 55 percent said that they had talked about those topics more frequently in the months since it began. "We were encouraged to see the real impact the #MeToo movement is having among young people," said MTV researcher Noopur Agarwal. "They are re-examining past behavior, re-thinking the way they approach romantic relationships, and noticing others changing around them. These shifts really help underscore the power of real stories and open dialogue" (Lusinski 2018).

Some women approached dating more cautiously after seeing a seemingly endless stream of #MeToo stories in the news or in their social media feeds. For survivors of sexual assault, the #MeToo revelations sometimes triggered unpleasant memories of traumatic incidents from the past. Other women felt overwhelmed or frightened by the prevalence of sexual misconduct, which made dating seem like a dangerous endeavor. On the other hand, many women felt empowered by the #MeToo reckoning. They saw women's concerns being taken seriously, which gave them greater confidence that the men they dated would treat them with respect.

The #MeToo movement left many men feeling uncertain, confused, and hesitant about how to proceed in the realm of dating and relationships. As women spoke out about their experiences, it forced many men to look back on their own behavior in a new way. According to the MTV survey, one-third of young male respondents expressed concern that something they had done in the past could be perceived as sexual harassment (Lusinski 2018). In the post-#MeToo dating landscape, men worried about recognizing social cues, crossing boundaries, having their actions misinterpreted, and being accused of behaving inappropriately. "#MeToo has done a tremendous job of breaking barriers and exposing some of the most horrid offenders, but in some ways, it has created a culture of 'guilty until proven innocent,'" Brendan Pringle argued in the *Washington Examiner*. "Any woman can claim that a man has 'harassed' her, and people are inclined to accept it as true without any proof whatsoever. Generally speaking, this has caused men on the dating scene to tread ultra-cautiously" (Pringle 2018).

Some critics charged that the #MeToo movement "inadvertently fostered a culture of fear in the dating scene" by creating confusion about appropriate conduct (Petter 2018). The MTV survey revealed that 68 percent of young people felt unclear about what behaviors constituted sexual harassment (Lusinski 2018). This uncertainty made people less inclined to approach and interact with one another for fear of breaking the rules or causing offense. Some critics claimed that #MeToo had a "chilling effect" on dating by making it dull, businesslike, superficial, and politically correct (Paul 2018). They complained about a loss of spontaneity and romance, such as when couples felt the need to ask permission before engaging in their first kiss. "In the #MeToo era, it seems that millennials have fallen victim to their own wokeness and catchy social media hashtags," Pringle asserted (Pringle 2018).

Changing Attitudes and Behaviors

#MeToo supporters dismissed critics' concerns about the movement's impact on romantic relationships as overblown. They viewed the re-examination of men's past behavior as a positive development that had the potential to make dating safer and more equitable in the future. They also asserted that communication could help men and women establish boundaries and avoid inappropriate dating behavior. "It is pretty easy to know what actions would constitute sexual harassment," said one writer. "If you analyze situations and are aware of your own character in any way, you don't really accidentally do any of these things. If you are trying to build a better relationship with all of this happening the key is communication" (Paul 2018).

#MeToo supporters suggested a variety of good dating practices to help men avoid crossing the line into sexual misconduct. One important practice, as Ansari's experience demonstrated, involves paying attention to non-verbal signals indicating that a woman may not reciprocate romantic interest or welcome sexual advances, such as avoiding eye contact, appearing uncomfortable or nervous, and moving away from a physical touch. Verbal cues may also provide insight into a partner's state of mind during a date or sexual encounter. If a partner's comments indicate hesitation or displeasure, even in an indirect or ambiguous way, asking questions and obtaining verbal permission is the safest and most respectful way to proceed. "Our bodies are zoned," Laura Kipnis explained in the *Guardian*. "There are public areas and private ones; parts you can touch without permission, such as my hand, and parts you're trespassing if you encroach on them without my permission" (Kipnis 2018).

The #MeToo movement generated significant debate about the concept of consent. For sexual activity to be considered consensual, both parties must willingly and deliberately give their approval to participate. In relationships between men and women, #MeToo activists pointed out, the balance of power is often weighted toward men, whether due to workplace status or physical strength. This unequal power dynamic has implications for consent. If a woman participates in sexual activity to avoid career repercussions or physical danger, her participation may be voluntary but not consensual. #MeToo activists noted that men can avoid such situations by repeatedly seeking affirmative consent as well as explicitly offering their sexual partners permission to say no. Open communication provides both parties in dating relationships with assurances that their feelings and expressions are reciprocated.

Further Reading

Framke, Caroline. 2018. "The Controversy around Babe.net's Aziz Ansari Story, Explained." *Vox*, January 17. https://www.vox.com/culture/2018/1/17/16897440/aziz-ansari-allegations-babe-me-too

Kipnis, Laura. 2018. "Has #MeToo Gone Too Far, or Not Far Enough? The Answer Is Both." *Guardian*, January 13. https://www.theguardian.com/commentisfree/2018/jan/13/has-me-too-catherine-deneuve-laura-kipnis

Lusinski, Natalia. 2018. "How #MeToo Is Affecting Young People's Dating Lives, according to a New Survey." *Bustle*, January 22. https://www.bustle.com/p/how-me-too-is-affecting-young-peoples-dating-lives-according-to-a-new-survey-7964470

Paul, Kari. 2018. "Young Single Americans Are Tired, Confused, and Scared about Dating during #MeToo." *MarketWatch*, March 6. https://www.market watch.com/story/young-single-americans-are-tired-confused-and-scared-about-dating-during-metoo-2018-02-27

Petter, Olivia. 2018. "How to Date during the #MeToo Era." *Independent*, April 23. https://www.independent.co.uk/life-style/love-sex/dating-me-too-era-rules-sexual-harassment-flirting-a8314876.html

Pringle, Brendan. 2018. "#MeToo Complicates Dating for Millennials." *Washington Examiner*, February 14. https://www.washingtonexaminer.com/metoo -effect-complicates-dating-for-millennials

Way, Katie. 2018. "I Went on a Date with Aziz Ansari. It Turned into the Worst Night of My Life." *Babe*, January 13. https://babe.net/2018/01/13/aziz -ansari-28355

Weiss, Bari. 2018. "Aziz Ansari Is Guilty. Of Not Being a Mind Reader." *New York Times*, January 18. https://www.nytimes.com/2018/01/15/opinion/aziz -ansari-babe-sexual-harassment.html

Assessing Men's Apologies for Past Harassment

With the rise of the #MeToo movement in the fall of 2017, dozens of powerful men in the worlds of academia, business, entertainment, media, and politics faced allegations of sexual harassment or assault. Many men responded to the accusations by issuing public apologies for their past behavior. Some observers of the #MeToo movement's cultural fallout analyzed the apologies, critiquing their content, tone, and likely impact on victims' feelings and the broader conversation about sexual misconduct. While a few of the apologies received praise for seeming heartfelt and sincere, many others met with criticism for appearing disingenuous or conditional. "They're sleazy, self-serving, vague, mind-bending, gaslighting," said psychologist Harriet Lerner, author of *Why Won't You Apologize? Healing Big Betrayals and Everyday Hurts*. "There's no accountability, and they make every apology mistake that one could make" (Orso 2017).

Experts note that apologies, when handled well, have the potential to aid the healing process for victims of sexual harassment. Honest, heartfelt apologies confirm the accuracy of their accounts, acknowledge their injuries, and provide the opportunity for closure on their traumatic experiences. Public apologies also offer potential benefits to society by sparking public debate, demonstrating the pervasiveness of the problem, and making it easier for victims to come forward in the future.

When apologies are handled poorly, however, they give perpetrators a platform to present their viewpoint and excuse their behavior while minimizing the experiences of survivors and making them feel silenced. Rather than healing wounds, insincere nonapologies can promote victim-blaming and make it more difficult for victims to come forward. "Humans are wired for defensiveness," Lerner stated. "It's very hard for us to take clear and direct responsibility for specific things we have said or done—or not said or done—without a hint of blaming, obfuscation, excuse-making [or] bringing up the other person's crime sheet" (Ulaby 2017).

Good and Bad Apologies

According to sociologist David Karp, good apologies must include a clear, specific statement of the wrongdoing and harm caused. Many of the public apologies offered by celebrities in response to #MeToo disclosures made only vague, generalized references to their inappropriate conduct. For example, Hollywood producer Harvey Weinstein said "I appreciate the way I've behaved with colleagues in the past has caused a lot of pain," while television journalist Charlie Rose said "I have behaved insensitively at times" (North 2017).

Scholars of human behavior assert that in addition to including explicit admissions of guilt and acknowledgments of responsibility, good apologies are given without conditions, qualifications, or denials. Victims of sexual harassment or assault emphasize that their abusers need to take full ownership of their actions. "When men say sorry, it shouldn't be shrouded in, 'I was young and stupid and drunk' or 'I had no idea' or 'I misread the signals,'" said one victim. "It should be a full admission that they behaved in a way that they see now was hurtful and/or damaging" (Fetters 2018).

In January 2018, for example, Dan Harmon, creator of the television show *Community*, used his own podcast to issue a public apology to *Community* writer Megan Ganz for his "selfish," "cowardly," and "cruel" behavior toward her after she rejected his romantic advances. "What's refreshing [about his apology]," wrote journalist Marissa Martinelli, "is that Harmon explains the ways he thought and acted at the time without making excuses or throwing himself a pity party. Instead, he uses the entire experience to urge others to consider their own actions and attitudes toward women in the workplace." For her part, Ganz publicly forgave Harmon for what he himself described as months of "creeping" on her. She even described his remarks as a "masterclass in How to Apologize" (Martinelli 2018).

In his apology, Democratic Senator Al Franken of Minnesota discussed a particular photograph in which he appeared to be grabbing the breasts of a female entertainer during a 2006 USO tour. Franken accepted responsibility, validated the woman's feelings, and expressed remorse. "I don't know what was in my head when I took that picture, but that doesn't matter," he wrote. "There's no excuse and I understand why you could feel violated by that photo" (Ulaby 2017). By affirming their victims' credibility, these men increased the likelihood that the public would believe women who came forward in the future.

In many cases, however, statements issued by men accused of sexual harassment have minimized the harm caused by their behavior or challenged the accuracy of the charges leveled against them. Television journalist Matt

Lauer qualified his apology by saying, "Some of what is being said about me is untrue or mischaracterized, but there is enough truth in these stories to make me feel embarrassed and ashamed." Similarly, Mark Halperin of ABC News stated, "In almost every case, I have recognized conduct for which I feel profound guilt and responsibility," but added that "some of the allegations that have been made against me are not true" (North 2017). Partial denials raise doubts about the veracity of accusers' reports, leaving the public to debate about which elements are true or false.

Other prominent men accused of sexual misconduct have made excuses or attempted to deflect public attention away from the allegations. Weinstein claimed that his attitudes toward women had simply failed to keep up with changing times. "I came of age in the '60s and '70s, when all the rules about behavior and workplaces were different," he wrote (Orso 2017). Spokespeople for former president George H. W. Bush, who was accused of groping women during photo opportunities, claimed that the women misunderstood his actions. "At age 93, President Bush has been confined to a wheelchair for roughly five years, so his arm falls on the lower waist of people with whom he takes pictures," the statement read (Orso 2017). Radio host Garrison Keillor insisted that his hand accidentally slipped inside a colleague's blouse as he patted her back. He also discounted the woman's feelings by claiming that at least 100 women had allowed their hands to "drift down below the beltline" while taking selfies with him over the years (Silva 2017).

One of the public apologies that generated the most intense criticism came from actor Kevin Spacey, who was accused of molesting actor Anthony Rapp and several other young men. Spacey claimed not to remember the incident, speculated that he must have been drunk, and then cast doubt on Rapp's report by stating, "If I did behave then as he describes, I owe him the sincerest apology" (Silva 2017). Spacey concluded his statement by coming out as gay, thus diverting media attention away from the past allegations and shifting it to his revelation about his sexual orientation. He came under fire from many people in the LGBTQ community for conflating sexual misconduct with homosexuality and thus contributing to stereotypes of gay men as sexual predators.

Many famous men also made the mistake of expecting their apologies to result in forgiveness and the restoration of their reputations and careers. Experts contend that apologies made in good faith should never demand forgiveness or request anything else from the harmed party. Weinstein committed that error by asking for a "second chance" in the film industry (North 2017). Advocates for women emphasize that the act of apologizing for sexual harassment and other misconduct does not guarantee absolution. Instead, the victim has the right to determine whether and when to accept an apology and forgive an offense.

Another common mistake made by famous men in #MeToo apologies involved self-promotion. Many accused men flattered themselves by declaring their respect for women, citing their credentials as a feminist ally, or mentioning their support for gender equality. Weinstein's statement, for instance, made note of the scholarship fund he established for women interested in studying film direction. "Basically, it's a performance," Lerner stated. "It's an act of self-protection, an attempt to do damage control, to save one's reputation" (Ulaby 2017). Good apologies, on the other hand, avoid self-aggrandizement and express a genuine desire to make amends for past behavior and to make positive changes going forward.

Although many of the statements made in response to #MeToo allegations fell short of the requirements of a good apology, the critique surrounding them helped promote the goals of the movement by clarifying social expectations of behavior and establishing new public norms. "No apology will ever be completely pure. Self-interest—whether professional, financial, emotional, or spiritual—is always wired in," Katy Waldman wrote in *Slate*. "Perhaps the question is whether the listeners are ready to mend broken ties, to allow the apologizer to try to become a better person" (Waldman 2017).

Further Reading

Fetters, Ashley. 2018. "This Is How to Apologize for Sexual Misconduct." *Men's Health*, March 19. https://www.menshealth.com/trending-news/a19479480/sexual-misconduct-apology/

Lerner, Harriet. 2017. *Why Won't You Apologize? Healing Big Betrayals and Everyday Hurts*. New York: Simon and Schuster.

Martinelli, Marissa. 2018. "Dan Harmon Acknowledges That He Sexually Harassed *Community* Writer Megan Ganz in a Seven-Minute Podcast Monologue." *Slate*, January 11. https://slate.com/arts/2018/01/dan-harmon-apologizes-to-community-writer-megan-ganz-on-harmontown.html

North, Anna. 2017. "How to Apologize for Sexual Harassment." *Vox*, December 5. https://www.vox.com/identities/2017/12/5/16710430/sexual-harassment-apologies-matt-lauer-louis-ck

Orso, Anna. 2017. "The Anatomy of an Apology: 12 Public Statements Analyzed and Annotated." *Philadelphia Inquirer*, December 5. http://www.philly.com/philly/living/harvey-weinstein-matt-lauer-kevin-spacey-sexual-harassment-apology-20171204.html

Silva, Christianna. 2017. "The Worst #MeToo Apologies from Famous Men Accused of Sexual Harassment." *Newsweek*, December 1. http://www.newsweek.com/worst-apologies-metoo-men-sexual-misconduct-726631

Ulaby, Neda. 2017. "How to Apologize for Sexual Harassment (Hint: It Takes More Than 'Sorry')." NPR, November 22. https://www.npr.org/2017/11/22/565913664/how-to-apologize-for-sexual-harassment-hint-it-takes-more-than-sorry

Waldman, Katy. 2017. "Wasted Reckonings: What Do We Really Want Out of Public Apologies from Accused Sexual Harassers?" *Slate*, November 14. http://www.slate.com/articles/arts/culturebox/2017/11/what_do_we_want_from_public_apologies_by_accused_sexual_harassers_like_louis.html

CHAPTER FOUR

Profiles

This section provides illuminating biographical profiles of important figures in the #MeToo movement, from early voices such as Anita Hill and Tarana Burke to contemporary activists and leaders such as Ashley Judd, Rose McGowan, Terry Crews, and Susan Fowler.

Sarah Ballard (1984–)

Astronomer who raised awareness of sexual harassment in academia

Although Sarah Ballard enjoyed the challenge of mathematics during her high school years, she never envisioned herself becoming a scientist. Ballard entered the University of California at Berkeley with the intention of majoring in gender studies or conflict resolution and becoming a social worker. A freshman-level astronomy course changed the direction of her life. "What started as just a class to tolerate shifted very slowly to be my favorite class," she recalled. "I would sometimes get goosebumps in lecture because of how vast and incredible the universe is" (Meinbresse 2015).

Ballard earned a bachelor's degree in astrophysics from the University of California at Berkeley in 2007, followed by a doctorate in astronomy and astrophysics from Harvard University in 2012. After spending three years at the University of Washington as a National Aeronautics and Space Administration Carl Sagan Postdoctoral Fellow, she moved to the Massachusetts Institute of Technology as a Torres Fellow for Exoplanetary Research in 2015. Ballard specializes in exoplanetary astrophysics, a field of academic study that focuses on planets orbiting stars other than the Sun. After astronomers discovered the first exoplanet in 1995, they developed and refined techniques that allowed them to identify thousands more planets. Ballard used the transit-timing variation method to analyze photographic data from the NASA Kepler space telescope. Her work resulted in the discovery of four exoplanets, known as Kepler-19b, Kepler-19c, Kepler-61b, and Kepler-93b. Her team produced precise measurements of Kepler-93b and determined that its diameter was smaller than that of Earth.

As she built her career in astronomy, Ballard studied and worked with some of the most prominent scientists in her field. In 2005, as a 21-year-old undergraduate at Berkeley, she took a course taught by Geoff Marcy, a world-renowned pioneer in exoplanetary research whose name was often mentioned among candidates for the Nobel Prize. When Marcy attended a Take Back the Night rally against sexual violence that she organized, Ballard sent the famous astronomer an email to thank him for supporting her cause. Marcy responded by providing his home phone number and encouraging her to call him. "I felt very confused by that," Ballard recalled, "and I just pretended like I hadn't seen it" (Scoles 2016).

Ballard later began meeting Marcy outside of class to discuss her research, and she initially considered him a valuable mentor. "The fact that he was so encouraging to me made me feel really good about myself and made me feel hopeful about my future in astronomy," she stated (Scoles 2016). Her attitude changed, however, when Marcy began discussing inappropriate topics, such as having sex outdoors with a former girlfriend. The last straw came when he gave her a ride home, then reached across the car and began massaging the back of her neck. Feeling uncomfortable and frightened, Ballard jumped out of the car and ran into her apartment building. "For a long time, I really chastised myself for being so stupid as to get in his car," she acknowledged (Scoles 2016).

Ballard struggled to process her feelings of shame and confusion until 2011, when she attended a conference for women in astronomy and heard that other students had accused Marcy of behaving inappropriately. "I thought that it was only me," she said. "I was unsure of whether I had done something wrong. And so the fact that I later learned that it was a pattern of behavior meant I was able to contextualize what happened" (Scoles 2016). In 2014, Berkeley administrators launched a Title IX investigation into student sexual harassment complaints against Marcy. Ballard agreed to participate in hopes of protecting other young women. "I wanted to be the woman that I needed then," she explained. "Because I felt completely disempowered and afraid and confused. And I needed a woman who was older, or a person who had more familiarity with the lay of the landscape, to make it stop in some way. And I realized in 2014 that I was this woman" (Scoles 2016).

The university released its report in June 2015. It found the allegations by Ballard (known as Complainant 2) and three other students to be credible and determined that Marcy violated campus sexual harassment policies between 2001 and 2010. Rather than taking disciplinary action, however, the university warned Marcy not to touch or be alone with students in the future. Ballard and the other complainants felt frustrated that the university chose to protect a powerful professor rather than vulnerable students. "It was my first realization that the academic system that I thought was so meritorious, that I wanted to actually spend my life within, was deeply unfair," Ballard recalled. "I wouldn't receive any justice and he could go on and harass other women" (Stoynoff 2017).

In October 2015, Ballard and the other women took the story to the media. An article appeared in *BuzzFeed* detailing the Title IX findings and the university's response. The revelations generated outrage in the science community and launched a national discussion about the pervasiveness of sexual harassment in academia. Thousands of scientists across the country signed a petition calling for Marcy to be fired. He resigned from the Berkeley faculty a few days later and posted a public letter of apology on his website. Ballard, who allowed her name to be used in the article, emerged as a leading activist in the fight for gender equity in science. She pointed out that women received lower salaries and less grant money than men with the same qualifications and achievements. She also called for academic institutions to adopt parental leave policies to help women remain in science after starting families. Ballard joined panel discussions aimed at stopping sexual harassment in academia and hosted a podcast offering advice to women in science. In 2015, she received the L'Oreal USA for Women in Science Award, which provided $60,000 to support her ongoing postdoctoral research.

Further Reading

Ghorayshi, Azeen. 2015. "Famous Berkeley Astronomer Violated Sexual Harassment Policies over Many Years." *BuzzFeed*, October 9. https://www.buzzfeed.com/azeenghorayshi/famous-astronomer-allegedly-sexually-harassed-students

Meinbresse, Debbie. 2015. "3Q: Sarah Ballard on Astrophysics and Gender Equity in Science." *MIT News*, November 13. http://news.mit.edu/2015/3q-sarah-ballard-astrophysics-and-gender-equity-science-1113

Scoles, Sarah. 2016. "What Happens When a Harassment Whistleblower Goes on the Science Job Market." *Wired*, July 17. https://www.wired.com/2016/07/happens-harassment-whistleblower-goes-science-job-market/

Stoynoff, Natasha. 2017. "I Was Sexually Harassed by My Professor: After Years of Silent Struggle, Astronomer Sarah Ballard Tells Her Story." *People*, July 27.

https://people.com/human-interest/i-was-sexually-harassed-by-my
-professor-after-years-of-silent-struggle-astronomer-sarah-ballard-tells-her
-story/

Tarana Burke (1973–)

Civil rights activist and founder of the #MeToo movement

Tarana Burke was born on September 12, 1973, in the Bronx borough of
New York City. She grew up in a housing project in a low-income neighborhood. Although her family lacked financial resources, Burke learned the
value of community involvement and education from an early age. Her
mother enrolled her in youth programs and introduced her to literature
by such great African American writers as Maya Angelou, Zora Neale Hurs-
ton, and Toni Morrison. "Those were the things that helped change the trajectory of my life," Burke recalled (Brockes 2018). At the age of 14, Burke
joined the Twenty-First Century Youth Leadership Movement and trained
to become a grassroots organizer. In 1989, she organized a rally to protest
a media campaign financed by businessman Donald Trump that inflamed
public opinion against five young men of color wrongfully accused of raping a white female jogger in Central Park.

After earning a bachelor's degree from Auburn University, Burke became
involved in social justice work in Selma, Alabama. In 1997, Burke met a 13-
year-old girl who confided that she had been sexually assaulted by her
mother's boyfriend. In the moment, Burke struggled to come up with an
appropriate response to express support for the girl and let her know that
she was not alone. As a survivor of sexual abuse herself, Burke later realized
that she could have provided a powerful message of "empowerment
through empathy" by simply saying, "Me too." "On one side, it's a bold,
declarative statement that 'I'm not ashamed' and 'I'm not alone,' " she
explained. "On the other side, it's a statement from survivor to survivor that
says, 'I see you, I hear you, I understand you, and I'm here for you' " (Santiago 2017).

In 2003, Burke founded Just Be, Inc., a nonprofit organization focused
on improving the self-esteem and well-being of black girls between the ages
of 12 and 18. She developed a program to help disadvantaged girls overcome their circumstances and reach their potential. "We had some girls
there that were dealing with some really horrible stuff," she remembered.
"So, when I'd say that Oprah went through something at 14 *and still became
Oprah*, that's what opens up a conversation about life possibility. You can
change the trajectory of your life" (Jefferson 2018). Through her work,

Burke realized the prevalence of sexual violence in the girls' lives. In one group of 30 teenage girls, for instance, 20 reported having experienced unwanted sexual contact. In 2006, Burke began using the phrase "Me Too" in a grassroots campaign to promote healing among women of color who had experienced sexual violence or exploitation.

Over the next decade, Burke continued her social justice work in Philadelphia and New York City. In 2017, a series of female celebrities came forward with allegations of sexual misconduct against Hollywood film mogul Harvey Weinstein. On October 15, actress and activist Alyssa Milano responded to the Weinstein scandal by encouraging her Twitter followers to use the hashtag #MeToo if they had experienced sexual harassment or assault. The phrase went viral online, as millions of survivors around the world used it to share their personal stories. Burke initially panicked when she discovered that "Me Too" had been appropriated as the slogan of a broader movement. "I didn't know how I would be included in the narrative," she acknowledged. "I thought I'd be lost and I thought my work would be lost" (Jefferson 2018).

As soon as Milano learned the origin of the phrase, she reached out to Burke, and the two activists worked together to shape the burgeoning #MeToo movement. Burke stressed the importance of focusing on survivors, rather than perpetrators, and offering them resources and support to promote healing. Her role also involved amplifying marginalized voices that might not otherwise be heard. She pointed out that the media often highlighted the "Me Too" stories of celebrities and white women, although women of color and LGBTQ individuals were statistically more likely to experience sexual violence. "If these are the stories in Hollywood, imagine the stories that are in everyday communities," she stated. "We have to always assert ourselves and be aggressive about women being misrepresented. Is it only valid if CNN talks about it? Why isn't it valid when *we* talk about it?" (Jefferson 2018).

The expansion of the #MeToo movement gave Burke many new opportunities to share her message. *Time* magazine named her, Milano, and other "Silence Breakers" who helped raise awareness of sexual harassment and assault as its Person of the Year for 2017. In January 2018, actress Michelle Williams invited Burke to attend the Golden Globe Awards as her guest. Burke received the 2018 Ridenhour Prize for Courage in recognition of her work for social justice. She also told the story of her life and work in a memoir, *Here the Light Enters: The Founding of the Me Too Movement*, scheduled for publication in 2019. In addition to promoting the #MeToo movement, Burke serves as senior director of Girls for Gender Equity, a Brooklyn-based nonprofit organization aimed at ending discrimination based on race, gender, and class and providing equal opportunity for girls and women.

Further Reading

Brockes, Emma. 2018. "Me Too Founder Tarana Burke: 'You Have to Use Your Privilege to Serve Other People.'" *Guardian*, January 15. https://www .theguardian.com/world/2018/jan/15/me-too-founder-tarana-burke -women-sexual-assault

Garcia, Sandra E. 2017. "The Woman Who Created #MeToo Long before Hashtags." *New York Times*, October 20. https://www.nytimes.com/2017/10/20/ us/me-too-movement-tarana-burke.html

Jefferson, J'na. 2018. "A Long Road Ahead: #MeToo Founder Tarana Burke on Sexual Assault, Stigmas, and Society." *Vibe*, April 3. https://www.vibe.com/ featured/tarana-burke-me-too-feature/

Santiago, Cassandra, and Doug Criss. 2017. "An Activist, a Little Girl, and the Heartbreaking Origin of #MeToo." CNN, October 17. https://www.cnn.com/2017/ 10/17/us/me-too-tarana-burke-origin-trnd/index.html

Terry Crews (1968–)

First male actor to come forward with a Hollywood #MeToo story

Terry Alan Crews was born on July 30, 1968, in Flint, Michigan. His father, Terry Sr., worked as a foreman in a General Motors assembly plant, while his mother, Patricia, was a homemaker. Crews described his father as a violent alcoholic who beat his wife and terrorized his children. "I'm from one of the worst cities in America, from a dysfunctional family, an abusive dad—I have been digging out of a hole since I was four years old," he stated (Wilkinson 2018). Crews earned his high school diploma from the Flint Academy and attended the Interlochen Center for the Arts on an art scholarship. He went to college at Western Michigan University in Kalamazoo, where he joined the football team as a walk-on and played defensive end for the Broncos' 1988 Mid-American Conference championship squad. In 1990, Crews married Rebecca King, a singer, speaker, and television producer. They eventually had five children.

The Los Angeles Rams selected Crews in the 11th round of the 1991 National Football League (NFL) draft. His professional football career spanned seven seasons, during which he appeared in 32 games with five different NFL teams. In 1997, Crews retired from football and moved to Los Angeles in hopes of launching a career in the entertainment industry. He initially made ends meet by modeling and appearing in commercials and music videos. His break as an actor came in 2002, when he won a role in the comedy film *Friday after Next* with Ice Cube. Crews is probably best known for his roles on three popular television sitcoms: Julius Rock on

Everybody Hates Chris (2005–2009); Nick Kingston-Persons on *Are We There Yet?* (2010–2012); and Sergeant Terry Jeffords on *Brooklyn Nine-Nine* (2013–2018). His most recognizable film roles include action hero Hale Caesar in *The Expendables* and its sequels, and superhero Bedlam in *Deadpool 2*. In 2014, Crews published an autobiography entitled *Manhood: How to Be a Better Man—Or Just Live with One*.

Crews emerged as an activist in October 2017, after the *New York Times* published an article detailing allegations of sexual misconduct against Hollywood film producer Harvey Weinstein that helped launch the #MeToo movement. For Crews, the Weinstein scandal brought back memories of an incident that occurred in February 2016, when he and his wife attended a party hosted by actor Adam Sandler. A high-profile Hollywood agent, Adam Venit, allegedly made suggestive gestures with his tongue and then grabbed Crews's crotch. "He comes over to me. I stick my hand out, and he literally takes his hand and puts it and squeezes my genitals. I jump back like, 'Hey, hey,' " Crews remembered. "And he's still licking his tongue out and all this stuff, and I go, 'Dude, what are you doing? What are you doing?' and then he comes back again. He just won't stop." According to Crews, after he pushed Venit away, the agent stood there grinning at him. "He's one of the most powerful men in Hollywood," Crews noted, "and he looked at me at the end as if, 'Who is going to believe you?' " (Kindelan 2017).

Crews initially kept quiet about the incident. Once the flood of #MeToo revelations began, however, he felt compelled to share his story as a way of supporting other victims of sexual assault. "I saw my social media and men specifically were calling these women gold diggers and opportunists who just wanted a pay day," he explained. "And it had happened to me. I'm reading all these guys calling these women all these names and I was like: 'I can't let this happen.' I would have been the biggest farce ever. I'm just going to say what happened to me and let everybody else be the judge" (Bernstein 2018). On October 10, Crews described his experience in a series of tweets. His disclosures quickly went viral, and he became the most prominent male voice in the growing #MeToo movement.

Crews argued that men have a responsibility to speak out against sexual abuse and advocate for women's rights. "Men need to hold other men accountable," he stated. "I came up in the cult of masculinity, in football and the sports world and entertainment. You're in places and guys are saying the wildest things. People need to be called on that. You need to be held accountable for the things you say, the things you do. What it came from is literally a belief that as a man you are more valuable than a woman" (Dockterman 2017). Some men criticized Crews for not using his physical strength to defend himself against the alleged assault. He insisted that a violent response would have made the situation worse. "If I would have just retaliated in defense, I would be under the jail right now. That's one thing I knew, that being a large African-American man in America, I would immediately be seen as a thug," he said. "But I'm not a thug. I'm an artist" (Kindelan 2017). In recognition of his courage in speaking out against sexual violence, *Time* magazine featured Crews among the "Silence Breakers" its editors named as Person of the Year for 2017. In June 2018, Crews testified before the U.S. Senate in support of the Sexual Assault Survivors' Bill of Rights.

Further Reading

Bernstein, Jonathan. 2018. "Terry Crews: Marvel, Toxic Masculinity, and Life after #MeToo." *Guardian*, May 22. https://www.theguardian.com/culture/2018/may/22/terry-crews-marvel-toxic-masculinity-and-life-after-metoo

Crews, Terry. 2014. *Manhood: How to Be a Better Man—Or Just Live with One*. New York: Random House.

Dockterman, Eliana. 2017. "Terry Crews: 'Men Need to Hold Other Men Accountable.'" *Time*, December 7. http://time.com/5049671/terry-crews-interview-transcript-person-of-the-year-2017/

Kindelan, Katie, and Sabina Ghebremedhin. 2017. "Terry Crews Names Alleged Sexual Assaulter: 'I Will Not Be Shamed.'" ABC News, November 15. https://abcnews.go.com/Entertainment/terry-crews-names-alleged-sexual-assaulter-shamed/story?id=51146972

Wilkinson, Alissa. 2018. "'So That's What Gaslighting Feels Like': Terry Crews on #MeToo and Sorry to Bother You." *Vox*, June 30. https://www.vox.com/summer-movies/2018/6/29/17501522/terry-crews-interview-metoo-venit-sorry-to-bother-you

Rachael Denhollander (1985–)

First accuser to come forward in the Larry Nassar sexual abuse case

Rachael Denhollander was born as Rachael Joy Moxon in Kalamazoo, Michigan, in 1985. Throughout her childhood and early teen years, she competed as a gymnast with the Kalamazoo Gymnastics Club. In 2000, when she was 15 years old, Denhollander experienced lower back pain from her rigorous gymnastics training. On the recommendation of her coach, she went to see Dr. Larry Nassar, an osteopathic physician at Michigan State University (MSU). As the team doctor for the USA Gymnastics training program, Nassar treated Olympic athletes and built a reputation as a leading expert in his field.

During a series of five, one-hour-long appointments in MSU's sports medicine clinic, Denhollander grew increasingly uncomfortable with Nassar's treatment techniques, which included massaging her breasts and buttocks and inserting his fingers into her vagina and rectum. "He penetrated me, he groped me, he fondled me," she recalled. "And then he whispered questions about how it felt. He engaged in degrading and humiliating sex acts without my consent or permission" (Macur 2018). Denhollander noticed that the renowned doctor became sexually aroused while treating her. Although Denhollander's mother sat in the corner of the room during the treatments, Nassar positioned himself to obstruct her view.

Nassar's treatments left Denhollander feeling confused, embarrassed, violated, and afraid. Although she knew on some level that Nassar's behavior was wrong, she questioned her own judgment because he was such a respected figure in the gymnastics community. "It was not possible that he was a predator, it was not possible that he could be in intimate contact with young children without anyone being very sure everything was proper," she thought, "so it *had* to be my mistake" (Wells 2018). Denhollander also hesitated to come forward because she worried that authorities would dismiss her complaints. "I was very, very certain I would not be believed," she noted, "and my greatest fear was that he would be empowered to continue if I tried and failed" (Wells 2018).

Over the next 15 years, Denhollander earned a law degree from the Oak Brook College of Law, married Jacob Denhollander, had three children, and moved to Louisville, Kentucky. She also continued to struggle with the traumatic impact of Nassar's sexual abuse. She found that she distrusted doctors, for instance, and had trouble letting her obstetrician touch her during childbirth. As an attorney, however, Denhollander grew determined to build a case against Nassar to protect other young gymnasts from harm. She collected her medical records, consulted medical journals, and interviewed pelvic floor specialists to disprove Nassar's claim that his treatments were medically indicated. She also researched Michigan law and prepared a formal complaint charging that Nassar's behavior met the definition of first-degree criminal sexual misconduct. "I knew it was going to be a fight," she explained. "I had to present the absolutely strongest case possible because it was a medically and legally complex case because a doctor and alleged medical treatment was involved" (Kozlowski 2018).

Denhollander finally decided to come forward in August 2016, after reading an article in the *Indianapolis Star* about sexual abuse complaints within USA Gymnastics. She contacted the paper about Nassar, took a folder full of information to the MSU Police, and filed a Title IX complaint with the university. When the *Star* printed Denhollander's allegations on

September 12, Nassar denied the charges and several MSU and USA Gymnastics officials came to his defense. "They believed him over her because of who he was purported to be," said Assistant Attorney General Angela Povilaitis. "She was ridiculed, folks rallied behind him, they tried to discredit her, they signed a petition and supported him" (Kozlowski 2018).

Denhollander's poise and determination inspired dozens of other victims to come forward, and the resulting police investigation resulted in Nassar's arrest. In November 2017, Nassar pleaded guilty to 10 counts of first-degree criminal sexual conduct. During the sentencing phase of the trial, Ingham County Circuit Court Judge Rosemarie Aquilina allowed the survivors of Nassar's abuse to address the court. A total of 156 women spoke over seven days in January 2018, sharing tragic stories of abuse, angry words of retribution, and powerful messages of strength and healing. Denhollander spoke last and challenged the judge to impose the maximum sentence. "How much is a little girl worth?" she demanded. "How much priority should be placed on communicating that the fullest weight of the law will be used to protect another innocent child from the soul shattering devastation that sexual assault brings? I submit to you that these children are worth everything. Worth every protection the law can offer" (Denhollander 2018).

After sentencing Nassar to spend the rest of his life in prison, Aquilina praised Denhollander for her courage, describing her as a "five-star general" who "built an army of survivors." "You started a tidal wave. You made all of this happen. You made all of these voices matter," the judge stated. "You are the bravest person I have ever had in my courtroom" (Agerholm 2018). The repercussions of Nassar's conviction extended far beyond the courtroom. The scandal led to the resignation of U.S. Olympic Committee chief executive Scott Blackmun, all 18 members of the USA Gymnastics board of directors, MSU president Lou Anna Simon, MSU athletic director Mark Hollis, and MSU gymnastics coach Kathy Klages. In May 2018, the MSU Board of Regents agreed to pay $500 million to settle lawsuits filed by 332 former patients of Nassar, including Denhollander. In recognition of her role in raising awareness of sexual abuse, *Time* magazine named Denhollander among the world's 100 Most Influential People for 2018. In addition, she and her army of survivors received the Arthur Ashe Courage Award at the ESPYs.

Further Reading

Agerholm, Harriet. 2018. "Rachael Denhollander: Abused U.S. Gymnast Receives Standing Ovation in Court after Judge's Tribute to Her Courage." *Independent*, January 25. https://www.independent.co.uk/

news/world/americas/rachael-denhollander-standing-ovation-video-larry
-nassar-judge-aquilina-praise-a8177456.html

Denhollander, Rachael. 2018. "Read Rachael Denhollander's Full Victim Impact
Statement." CNN, January 30. https://www.cnn.com/2018/01/24/us/
rachael-denhollander-full-statement/index.html

Kozlowski, Kim. 2018. "Rachael Denhollander: The Voice That Began End of
Nassar." *Detroit News*, January 24. https://www.detroitnews.com/story/
news/local/michigan/2018/01/24/nassar-denhollander/109787862/

Macur, Juliet. 2018. "In Larry Nassar's Case, a Single Voice Eventually Raised an
Army." *New York Times*, January 28. https://www.nytimes.com/2018/01/
24/sports/rachael-denhollander-nassar-gymnastics.html

Wells, Kate. 2017. "MSU Report: Nassar Assaulted Girl Who Told Gymnastics Coach
about Abuse." Michigan Radio, March 22. http://michiganradio.org/post/
msu-report-nassar-assaulted-girl-who-told-gymnastics-coach-about-abuse

Moira Donegan (1990?–)

Creator of the "Media Men List" warning women of alleged sexual harassers

Moira Donegan launched her career as a writer in 2013, shortly after graduating from college. Her work has appeared in such publications as *n+1*, the *New Yorker*, the *London Review of Books*, and *Bookforum*. She also served as an assistant editor at the *New Republic* in 2017. In October of that year, the *New York Times* published an article containing allegations of sexual misconduct against Hollywood film mogul Harvey Weinstein. The disclosures by famous women in the entertainment industry brought national attention to workplace sexual harassment and encouraged millions of women around the world to share their own stories online using the hashtag #MeToo.

Donegan responded to the Weinstein scandal and #MeToo revelations by creating an "anonymous, crowdsourced" Google spreadsheet "that collected a range of rumors and allegations of sexual misconduct, much of it violent, by men in magazines and publishing." She intended for the document, known as the S***ty Media Men List, to serve as a modern-day "whisper network" to allow women in the industry to "share their stories of harassment and assault without being needlessly discredited or judged." Donegan viewed it as a tool that women could use to protect themselves against predatory men, and she added a disclaimer advising users to "take everything with a grain of salt" (Donegan 2018).

Donegan shared the spreadsheet only with a few colleagues in the publishing industry, but it went viral online in a matter of hours. With input from anonymous contributors, the Media Men List quickly grew to include more than 70 men's names, along with their places of employment and details of their alleged misconduct, which ranged from crude remarks and inappropriate text messages to groping and rape. "Watching the cells populate, it rapidly became clear that many of us had weathered more than we had been willing to admit to one another," Donegan recalled. "This solidarity was thrilling, but the stories were devastating. I realized that the behavior of a few men I had wanted women to be warned about was far more common that I had ever imagined" (Donegan 2018). Only 12 hours after creating the list, Donegan deactivated it online when she learned that a *BuzzFeed* reporter had written an article about it. "I realized that I had created something that had grown rapidly beyond my control," she acknowledged. "I was overwhelmed and scared" (Donegan 2018).

Despite her efforts to contain it, the list continued to circulate and generated tremendous controversy. Some critics called it irresponsible and unfair because it spread information based on anonymous reports. They argued that being listed could harm a man's reputation and career without affording him an opportunity to defend himself against the allegations. Other critics derided the list as an improper and ineffective response to sexual harassment complaints. They insisted that victims of workplace harassment should report the perpetrators to human resources or the police.

Supporters, on the other hand, argued that the list would positively impact the publishing industry. "If it forced employers to look into long-standing situations and take action, so be it," Margaret Sullivan wrote in the *Washington Post*. "If it caused a great many men to be put on guard—and hence more respectful in their dealings with female colleagues—that's all to the good" (Sullivan 2018). The Media Men List prompted several companies to investigate sexual harassment complaints against employees. A few prominent men who appeared on the list faced disciplinary action as a result of these investigations, including *Atlantic* literary critic Leon Wieseltier, *Paris Review* editor Lorin Stein, *New Republic* editor Hamilton Fish, and *GQ* political reporter Rupert Myers.

Even though her identity remained a secret, Donegan noted that "the fear of being exposed, and of the harassment that will inevitably follow, has dominated my life" (Donegan 2018). In early 2018, rumors began circulating that writer Katie Roiphe—known as a prominent critic of the #MeToo movement—planned to identify Donegan as the creator of the Media Men List in an upcoming article for *Harper's Magazine*. Many feminists criticized the decision to reveal Donegan's name, arguing that it could expose her to online harassment, derail her career, and threaten her physical safety. Several prominent women, including television director Lexi Alexander, publicly claimed responsibility for creating the list as a way of protecting Donegan and expressing solidarity with her cause. After receiving an inquiry about the list from a *Harper's Magazine* fact-checker, Donegan decided to reveal her own identity and explain her motivations in an essay for the *Cut*. After coming forward, Donegan became a prominent voice in the #MeToo movement.

Further Reading

Ciampaglia, Dante A. 2018. "Who Is Moira Donegan? Woman behind 'S***ty Media Men' List Comes Forward." *Newsweek*, January 11. http://www.newsweek.com/who-moira-donegan-woman-behind-shitty-media-men-list-was-little-known-writer-777682

Donegan, Moira. 2018. "I Started the Media Men List. My Name Is Moira Donegan." *Cut*, January 10. https://www.thecut.com/2018/01/moira-donegan-i-started-the-media-men-list.html

Grady, Constance. 2018. "The S***ty Media Men List, Explained." *Vox*, January 11. https://www.vox.com/culture/2018/1/11/16877966/shitty-media-men-list-explained

Sullivan, Margaret. 2018. "She Created a Document to Warn Women of Sexual Harassers. It's Haunted Her Ever Since." *Washington Post*, April 22. https://www.washingtonpost.com/lifestyle/style/she-created-a-document-to-warn-women-of-sexual-harassers-its-haunted-her-ever-since/2018/04/20/a39f9fa8-44a0-11e8-8569-26fda6b404c7_story.html?utm_term=.f70c5457e6f1

Susan Fowler (1991?–)

Software engineer who blew the whistle on sexual harassment in the tech industry

Susan J. Fowler was born around 1991 in rural Yarnell, Arizona. Her father worked as an evangelical preacher and traveling salesman, while her mother homeschooled Susan and her six siblings. Fowler described her childhood as "unconventional" and recalled that she eventually took charge of her own education. "I tried to read the classics, would go to the library a lot, tried to teach myself things. But I didn't really have any direction," she stated. "I really wished that I could just learn and do all the fun things and cool extracurriculars that I thought everybody else my age was doing" (Dowd 2017). After preparing for college entrance exams on her own, Fowler received a full scholarship to the University of Arizona. Administrators there discouraged her from taking advanced math courses, though, because she lacked the usual prerequisites. She then transferred to the University of Pennsylvania, where she earned a degree in physics.

After graduating from college, Fowler launched her career as a software engineer at technology start-up firms in California's Silicon Valley. In November 2015, she joined the rapidly expanding, $69 billion ride-sharing service Uber as a site reliability engineer (SRE). Recognizing technology's reputation as a male-dominated industry, Uber executives recruited Fowler by representing the company as woman-friendly. From her first days on the job, however, she encountered a misogynistic "bro culture" that tolerated gender discrimination and sexual harassment. As soon as Fowler completed training and joined a team, for instance, her manager allegedly began sending her offensive messages in which he discussed his sex life and propositioned her. "It was clear that he was trying to get me to have sex with him, and it was so clearly out of line that I immediately took screenshots of these chat messages and reported him to HR [human resources]," she recalled (Fowler 2017). Upper management refused to discipline the manager, however, since he was a "high performer," and it was supposedly his first offense.

Fowler quickly transferred to a different team at Uber, where she met female engineers who had previously filed sexual harassment complaints against the same manager. Fowler convinced the women to accompany her to human resources (HR) to show that the manager had engaged in a pattern of inappropriate behavior. Despite their collective insistence, however, HR still claimed that no problem existed. Undaunted, Fowler continued to document and report instances of sexism and gender discrimination throughout her employment at Uber. "I didn't really care if they branded me a troublemaker, because I hadn't gotten that far in my life and overcome all these things to get treated inappropriately," she explained. "I wasn't going to take it. I'd worked so hard. I deserved so much better. And I was like, 'No. That's not OK. You don't get to do that' " (Dowd 2018). Uber management responded by blaming her for the problems, denying her transfer requests, downgrading her performance reviews without notifying her, and threatening to fire her for complaining.

Fowler quit her job at Uber in December 2016 and accepted a new position with the online payment-processing company Stripe. Many other female employees found the atmosphere at Uber untenable as well, as Fowler watched the percentage of women in its 150-person SRE organization drop from 25 percent when she joined the company to 3 percent by the time she left. On February 19, 2017, Fowler recounted what she described as the "strange, fascinating, and slightly horrifying story" of her year at Uber in a 3,000-word blog post. Her account of her experiences went viral online and reverberated through Silicon Valley. Critics of the tech industry culture presented her story as evidence of systemic problems. They claimed that many of the leading tech firms fostered a toxic, misogynistic work environment in which venture capitalists and investors protected innovative "high performers" who engaged in sexual misconduct.

Fowler's blog post put Uber's management and business practices under intense scrutiny. The company hired a law firm headed by former U.S. attorney general Eric Holder to investigate the charges. On June 13, Holder released a report that confirmed Fowler's account and offered a series of recommendations for restructuring Uber's senior leadership and overhauling its culture. The scathing report blamed Uber's cofounder and CEO, Travis Kalanick, for perpetuating a hostile work environment for female employees. Faced with allegations about his own conduct, Kalanick stepped down as head of Uber a few days later. Fowler's blog post also encouraged other women to go public with complaints about sexism in the tech industry. These allegations led to an industry-wide crackdown on sexual harassment that ended the careers of other powerful men in Silicon Valley. "It's bigger than me, and it's bigger than Uber," Fowler said. "For the first time, women are able to come forward with their own stories and they are being heard and they are being believed. Most importantly, there have been real consequences for the perpetrators" (Bhuiyan 2017).

The fallout from Fowler's blog post extended far beyond Silicon Valley. The courage she displayed as a whistleblower inspired women in other industries to speak out against sexual harassment in the workplace. Her actions thus helped launch the #MeToo movement, which brought down many prominent men in politics, media, and entertainment in 2017. "I feel a sense of relief, and a great deal of optimism for our future," Fowler stated. "It seems to me that this year, our country finally stood up and said that awful treatment of women will not be tolerated" (Bhuiyan 2017). Fowler received a great deal of recognition for her role as a change agent, including Person of the Year honors from the *Financial Times* and *Time* magazine (along with other "Silence Breakers" who spoke out against sexual harassment). She also sold book and movie rights to her story.

Fowler used her celebrity to fight the use of forced arbitration—clauses in employment contracts that require newly hired workers to give up their right to sue the company and agree to settle any workplace disputes in secretive arbitration hearings. Critics charge that such clauses serve to silence victims of sexual misconduct, hide labor violations from public view, and entrench toxic workplace cultures. Fowler argued that ending forced arbitration "would be the biggest thing you could do to stop the cycle of harassment, discrimination and retaliation in the workplace" (Levin 2018). Fowler is married to Chad Rigetti, founder of the tech start-up Rigetti Quantum Computing, and she gave birth to a daughter in 2018.

Further Reading

Bhuiyan, Johana. 2017. "With Just Her Words, Susan Fowler Brought Uber to Its Knees." *Recode*, December 6. https://www.recode.net/2017/12/6/16680602/susan-fowler-uber-engineer-recode-100-diversity-sexual-harassment

Dowd, Maureen. 2017. "She's 26 and Brought Down Uber's CEO. What's Next?" *New York Times*, October 21. https://www.nytimes.com/2017/10/21/style/susan-fowler-uber.html

Fowler, Susan. 2017. "Reflecting on One Very, Very Strange Year at Uber." *Blog*, February 19. https://www.susanjfowler.com/blog/2017/2/19/reflecting-on-one-very-strange-year-at-uber

Hook, Leslie. 2017. "FT Person of the Year: Susan Fowler." *Financial Times*, December 11. https://www.ft.com/content/b4bc2a68-dc4f-11e7-a039-c64b1c09b482

Levin, Sam. 2018. "Susan Fowler's Plan after Uber? Tear Down the System That Protects Harassers." *Guardian*, April 11. https://www.theguardian.com/technology/2018/apr/11/susan-fowler-uber-interview-forced-arbitration-law

Anita Hill (1956–)

Law professor who accused Supreme Court nominee Clarence Thomas of sexual harassment

Anita Faye Hill was born on July 30, 1956, in Lone Tree, Oklahoma. She was the youngest of 13 children born into the farming family of Albert and Erma Hill. An outstanding student, Hill became the valedictorian of her high school class and went on to earn a degree in psychology from Oklahoma State University in 1977, and a law degree from Yale University in 1980. Following a brief stint at a law firm, Hill moved to Washington, D.C., and took a job as an attorney in the Civil Rights Office of the U.S. Department of Education. In 1982, her boss, attorney Clarence Thomas, became chairman of the Equal Opportunity Employment Commission (EEOC), the federal agency charged with enforcing civil rights laws regarding workplace discrimination. Hill accepted a position as an assistant to Thomas at the EEOC. She left in 1983 to become a professor of law, public policy, and women's studies at Oral Roberts University and then at the University of Oklahoma.

In 1991, after Justice Thurgood Marshall announced his retirement, Republican President George H.W. Bush nominated Thomas to the U.S. Supreme Court. While conducting a background check on the nominee, Federal Bureau of Investigation (FBI) agents contacted Hill to inquire about her experiences working for Thomas a decade earlier. Hill told the agents that Thomas had sexually harassed her during her employment at the

Department of Education and the EEOC. Although Hill was initially reluctant to come forward, she decided that her complaints about Thomas's workplace conduct were relevant, given the important position for which he was being considered. "My concern was that I had information about the fitness of an individual who was going to sit on the highest court of the land," she stated (Thompson 2011).

At first, it appeared as if Thomas would win confirmation easily. Shortly before the Senate voted on his nomination, however, the FBI background report containing Hill's interview was leaked to the press. When news of her sexual harassment accusations became public, the Senate Judiciary Committee launched a new round of hearings and invited Hill to testify. Hill appeared before the committee on October 11, 1991. In her testimony, she claimed that Thomas subjected her to a pattern of inappropriate remarks and offensive conduct in the workplace during the two years she worked for him. She accused Thomas of repeatedly asking her out on dates, commenting on her clothing or appearance, bragging about his sexual prowess, and discussing sex acts he had seen in pornographic films.

Millions of people watched on television as Hill recounted Thomas's alleged behavior in graphic detail. Following her prepared statement, Hill endured hours of intensive questioning by the 14 members of the Judiciary Committee—all of whom were white males. Republican committee members, in the interest of protecting Bush's conservative nominee, attacked Hill's credibility, questioned her motivations for coming forward, and insisted that she had misrepresented or misinterpreted Thomas's behavior. Democratic committee members, led by Chairman Joseph Biden, seemed reluctant to defend Hill or intervene in the Republicans' aggressive cross-examination.

Biden also came under criticism from feminists for failing to call witnesses who were available to corroborate Hill's testimony—either friends whom she had told about Thomas's behavior or coworkers who had also experienced it. "These were not individuals who came forward because I'd contacted them and requested them to come forward," Hill said. "These are women who came forward on their own. It was shocking for all of us that they were not going to be called. And it left me to, as they say, carry the water on the issue alone" (Gordy 2011). Thomas denied Hill's allegations and angrily claimed that they were part of a racist conspiracy to deny him a spot on the court. The combative hearings ultimately turned on the question of whether Hill or Thomas was telling the truth. A majority of senators believed Thomas, and they voted 52–48 to confirm his lifetime appointment to the Supreme Court.

Hill stepped out of the spotlight and resumed her career in academia. Yet her appearance at the hearings had a lasting impact on American politics and culture. Many women resented the all-male committee's aggressive questioning of Hill and admired her poise and courage. Some supporters grew determined to change the atmosphere by electing more women to political office. The 1992 election became known as the "Year of the Woman," as the number of female members in the U.S. Congress increased from 30 to 51. In addition, Hill's testimony raised public awareness of sexual harassment in the workplace and empowered women to come forward. As a result, the number of sexual harassment claims filed with the EEOC more than doubled over the next five years. "I did not intend for it to become a referendum with regard to the issue of sexual harassment," Hill said. "But I think it was a topic that had been held in secret and shame for women, and then we were finally able to talk about it" (Gordy 2011).

In 1996, Hill accepted a teaching position at Brandeis University in Waltham, Massachusetts. The following year, she published an autobiography, *Speaking Truth to Power*, that offered her perspective on the controversial hearings. Hill returned to the news in 2013, when Academy Award-winning director Freida Mock told her story in the documentary film *Anita*. In 2016, the HBO movie *Confirmation* provided a dramatized version of the Thomas–Hill hearings, starring Kerry Washington as Hill. The emergence of the #MeToo movement in 2017 brought renewed attention to issues of workplace discrimination and sexual harassment. Many activists credited Hill for being one of the first women to speak out about these issues a quarter-century earlier. "In today's atmosphere, there would be more people who would understand my story, who would believe my story, and I think the numbers have changed over the year in terms of people who believe me and support me," Hill noted. "We cannot underestimate the impact that those hearings had, even though the vote did not go the way most of us wanted" (Lopez 2017).

In recognition of Hill's leading role in the fight against sexual harassment, Time's Up activists selected her to chair the Commission on Sexual Harassment and Advancing Equality in the Workplace, an organization dedicated to ending discriminatory and abusive practices in the entertainment industry. Hill appreciated that her actions left a legacy. "I don't think of 1991 and 2017 as isolated moments in history," she stated. "I see them as part of an arc, and an arc that has been bending towards justice" (Lopez 2017).

Further Reading

Gordy, Cynthia. 2011. "Anita Hill Defends Her Legacy." *Root*, October 20. https://www.theroot.com/anita-hill-defends-her-legacy-1790866401

Hill, Anita F. 1997. *Speaking Truth to Power*. New York: Doubleday.

Lopez, Ricardo. 2017. "Anita Hill on Sexual Harassment: 'Today, More People Would Believe My Story.'" *Variety*, December 8. https://variety.com/2017/biz/news/anita-hill-uta-sexual-harassment-1202634689/

Thompson, Krissah. 2011. "For Anita Hill, the Clarence Thomas Hearings Haven't Really Ended." *Washington Post*, October 11. https://www.washington post.com/politics/for-anita-hill-the-clarence-thomas-hearings-havent-really -ended/2011/10/05/gIQAy2b5QL_story.html?utm_term=.6315b3c7ff9a

Adama Iwu (1977?–)

Lobbyist who exposed pervasive sexual harassment in California politics

Born around 1977, Adama Iwu grew up in San Diego, California. She earned a bachelor's degree in political science from the University of San Diego in 2005, as well as a master's degree in public administration from California State University at Sacramento in 2006. Iwu worked as a government affairs representative for Advance America and Farmers Insurance before joining Visa in 2015 as the head of government relations in the western United States. Three years later, she became vice president of state government and community relations for Visa.

As a lobbyist, Iwu spent much of her time interacting with legislators at the California State Capitol in Sacramento. She also represented Visa's business interests to politicians at many corporate and social events. Some of these events assumed the permissive atmosphere of a fraternity party, and Iwu often encountered inappropriate behavior by male colleagues over the years. She felt powerless to address the behavior, though, without harming her career. "Men feel they have the right to grab you, tell really lewd stories in front of you," Iwu stated. "In order to be trusted and be part of the crowd, you have to act like one of the boys. So you laugh off lewd jokes, you laugh off sexual innuendos, you make excuses for men" (Megerian 2017).

In the fall of 2017, allegations of sexual misconduct against Hollywood film producer Harvey Weinstein brought national attention to the mistreatment of women in the workplace. The disclosures by well-known women in the entertainment industry encouraged millions of women around the world to share their own stories online using the hashtag #MeToo. In this environment of increasing awareness and decreasing tolerance for sexual harassment, Iwu claimed that a drunken male colleague assaulted her at a work function. After she greeted the man, she alleged that he repeatedly kissed and groped her despite her protests. To make matters worse, the incident occurred in front of several other men whom she considered good friends, but none of the witnesses intervened. "It enraged me that it happened in front of other male colleagues," Iwu recalled. "They said 'Oh, you hugged him, we thought you knew him.' That doesn't mean when I spent the other three minutes pushing him off me that I didn't want someone to step in and say 'She said no, stop'" (Luna 2017).

Iwu expressed her outrage and frustration about the incident in a text message to a friend. Before long, their conversation expanded to include dozens of other women working in politics who had experienced uncomfortable situations with male colleagues. Iwu decided to voice their concerns about the culture of sexual harassment and discrimination in state government by drafting an open letter to the *Los Angeles Times*. Known as the "We Said Enough" letter, the bipartisan missive appeared in the paper on October 17, 2017, with the signatures of nearly 150 female legislators, staff members, political consultants, and lobbyists attached. "Inappropriate, sexually harassing behavior cuts across every industry and facet of our society," the letter stated. "Each of us has endured, or witnessed, or worked with women who have experienced some form of dehumanizing behavior by men with power in our workplaces.... We're done with this. Each of us who signed this op-ed will no longer tolerate the perpetrators or enablers who do" (Iwu 2017).

The letter did not make accusations against specific individuals. Instead, it focused on changing the culture of state government to prevent sexual harassment from occurring. "Even if I was to say, 'Here's five men that everybody knows are a problem,' that doesn't actually fix the problem," Iwu explained (Mason 2017). In November 2017, Iwu and other signers were invited to testify before the Subcommittee on Harassment, Discrimination, and Retaliation convened by the California State Assembly to investigate the problem of sexual harassment in government. Several women came forward with allegations of sexual misconduct against sitting legislators, which resulted in the resignation of Democratic state assemblymen Raul Bocanegra and Matt Dababneh and Democratic state senator Tony Mendoza. Twenty-two other states conducted similar hearings that led to the adoption of reforms aimed at increasing accountability for perpetrators and protections for victims of sexual harassment.

Iwu and her supporters established an organization, We Said Enough, which collects women's stories of sexual violence on its website and provides survivors with access to legal services and other resources. As president of the board of We Said Enough, Iwu introduced a mobile app designed to improve the process of reporting sexual violence and supporting victims. In recognition of her campaign to expose sexual harassment in politics, *Time* magazine named Iwu among the "Silence

Breakers" who received the 2017 Person of the Year honor. Iwu appeared on the cover of the December 18 issue alongside actress Ashley Judd, singer Taylor Swift, Uber engineer Susan Fowler, and agricultural worker Isabel Pascual.

Further Reading

Iwu, Adama. 2017. "Women in California Politics Call Out 'Pervasive' Culture of Sexual Harassment." *Los Angeles Times*, October 17. http://documents .latimes.com/women-california-politics-call-out-pervasive-culture-sexual -harassment/

Luna, Taryn, and Alexei Koseff. 2017. "Campaign Grows against Sexual Harassment at California Capitol." *Sacramento Bee*, October 20. http://www.sacbee.com/ news/politics-government/capitol-alert/article179882956.html

Mason, Melanie. 2017. "Female Lawmakers, Staffers, and Lobbyists Speak Out on 'Pervasive' Harassment in California's Capitol." *Los Angeles Times*, October 17. http://www.latimes.com/politics/la-pol-ca-women-harassment-capitol -20171017-story.html

Megerian, Chris, Melanie Mason, Dakota Smith, and Jack Dolan. 2017. "In Her Own Words: Women of California Politics Tell Their Stories of Sexual Harassment and Unwanted Touching." *Los Angeles Times*, October 29. http://www .latimes.com/politics/la-pol-ca-sexual-harassment-sacramento-2017-htmlstory .html

Ashley Judd (1968–)

Actress and activist whose accusations launched the Weinstein scandal

Ashley Judd was born as Ashley Tyler Ciminella on April 19, 1968, in Los Angeles, California. Her father, Michael Ciminella, was a marketing analyst, and her mother, Naomi Judd, was a nurse who later became a successful country music singer. When her parents divorced in 1972, Judd moved to rural Kentucky with her mother and older half-sister, Wynonna. For the next decade, the family struggled financially and sometimes lived without plumbing or electricity.

In 1983, Naomi and Wynonna formed a mother–daughter recording duo, the Judds, and launched a successful career in the country music industry. The Judds began performing all over the country, leaving Ashley behind with various friends and relatives. Judd ended up attending more than a dozen different schools in her youth, and she often felt lonely, neglected, and vulnerable. "We came from a dysfunctional family system that didn't work very well," she noted. "So the kinds of things that happened to me are very typical and standard and indicative of a family system that doesn't work very well" (Inbar 2011).

After completing a degree in French from the University of Kentucky, Judd went to Hollywood in 1990 with hopes of becoming an actress. After landing a series of small roles on television, she received her big break as the title character in the 1993 independent film *Ruby in Paradise*, which won the Grand Jury Prize at the Sundance Film Festival. During the remainder of the 1990s, she played the leading role in several thrillers that achieved box-office success, including *Kiss the Girls* and *Double Jeopardy*. In the 2000s, Judd shifted toward roles in family-oriented films, such as *Divine Secrets of the Ya-Ya Sisterhood*, *Tooth Fairy*, and *Dolphin Tale*.

Beginning around 2004, Judd emerged as an outspoken "feminist social justice humanitarian," according to her website. Her activism focused on issues involving public health, human rights, women's equality, and environmental protection. She served as a global ambassador for the United Nations Population Fund, Population Services International, and YouthAIDS, working with these organizations to support family planning, reproductive health services, and AIDS prevention. Judd also helped combat human trafficking and modern-day slavery as an advisory board member for the Polaris Project, Demand Abolition, and Apne Aap Worldwide. She also worked to raise awareness of the environmental and health threats associated with the practice known as mountaintop-removal coal mining. Judd's commitment to charitable causes drove her to earn a master's degree in public administration from Harvard University's Kennedy School of Government in 2010, and then to begin work toward a doctoral degree from the Goldman School of Public Policy at the University of California, Berkeley.

In October 2015, Judd made headlines by disclosing in *Variety* magazine that "I was sexually harassed by one of our industry's most famous, admired-slash-reviled bosses" (Setoodeh 2015). Two years later, she publicly identified the man as producer Harvey Weinstein in an exposé published in the *New York Times*. The alleged incident occurred in 1997, when Judd was a relatively unknown actress appearing in *Kiss the Girls*. She claimed that Weinstein invited her to a breakfast meeting in his hotel room to discuss her career, answered the door in a bathrobe, and persistently requested sexual favors. "I said no, a lot of ways, a lot of times, and he always came back at me with some new ask," she recalled. "It was all this bargaining, this coercive bargaining" (Kantor and Twohey 2017). Judd said she eventually managed to escape by telling Weinstein that she would consider his requests once she won an Academy Award in one of his movies. "I felt bad about myself initially for the way I maintained my safety and got out of the room," she noted, "when, in fact, what I did was exceedingly clever and brilliant and self-preserving" (Setoodeh 2015).

In the weeks after the *New York Times* article appeared, more than 80 other women came forward to accuse Weinstein of sexual harassment or assault. Many of the complaints involved young, aspiring actresses and models who attended what they thought were professional meetings to discuss career opportunities, only to be subjected to unwanted sexual advances by the powerful producer. The disclosures by Judd and other celebrities encouraged millions of ordinary working women around the world to share their own stories online using the hashtag #MeToo. Judd received praise for being among the first Weinstein accusers to speak publicly, yet she insisted that she had never kept quiet about her experience. "I've told this story from literally the moment I left that hotel room with Harvey," she stated. "My dad was with me that day, and he could tell by the look on my face, to use his words, that something devastating had happened, and I told him. And both the producer and director of *Kiss the Girls* said recently that when I went to the set that night, I told them what had happened. I've been telling this story—but the seismic shift is that now everyone is willing to hear it" (Hayek 2018).

In recognition of her advocacy on behalf of victims of sexual harassment, *Time* magazine named Judd, along with other "Silence Breakers," as its Person of the Year for 2017. In April 2018, Judd filed a defamation lawsuit against Weinstein, charging that he retaliated against her for rejecting his sexual advances by spreading false rumors that harmed her career. Director Peter Jackson supported her case by saying that Weinstein urged him not to cast Judd in his blockbuster *Lord of the Rings* trilogy. Judd also emerged as a leading voice in the Time's Up movement, which aimed to develop actionable plans to eliminate workplace sexual harassment. "Part of why the movement has such guts and teeth is that we're writing codes of conduct that will be across our industry, across all the unions and agencies," she said. "Meetings happen between 9 a.m. and 6 p.m., they happen in an office, they happen with at least one other person present. No more of this meeting in hotel rooms, no more meeting at homes—it's over" (Hayek 2018).

Further Reading

Hayek, Salma. 2018. "Ashley Judd Is Reclaiming Her Time." *Town and Country*, March 1. https://www.townandcountrymag.com/leisure/arts-and-culture/a18729402/ashley-judd-interview-salma-hayek-april-2018/

Inbar, Michael. 2011. "Ashley Judd Reveals Troubled Childhood, Sexual Abuse."
     Today, April 5. https://www.today.com/popculture/ashley-judd-reveals
     -troubled-childhood-sexual-abuse-2D80556311
Judd, Ashley, and Maryanne Vollers. 2011. *All That Is Bitter and Sweet.* New York:
     Ballantine.
Kantor, Jodi, and Megan Twohey. 2017. "Harvey Weinstein Paid Off Sexual
     Harassment Accusers for Decades." *New York Times*, October 5.
     https://www.nytimes.com/2017/10/05/us/harvey-weinstein-harassment
     -allegations.html
The Official Website of Ashley Judd. 2017. "Biography." http://ashleyjudd.com/
     about/
Setoodeh, Ramin. 2015. "Ashley Judd Reveals Sexual Harassment by Studio
     Mogul." *Variety*, October 6. https://variety.com/2015/film/news/ashley
     -judd-sexual-harassment-studio-mogul-shower-1201610666/

Rose McGowan (1973–)

*Women's rights advocate and vocal opponent of sexism in the entertainment
industry*

Rose Arianna McGowan was born on September 5, 1973, in Florence,
Italy. Her American parents, Daniel and Terri McGowan, belonged to the
Children of God cult at the time of her birth. McGowen spent her childhood on a commune in Tuscany, where cult members beat her for not sharing their religious fervor. When McGowan was 10 years old, her family
escaped the cult, returned to the United States, and settled in the Pacific
Northwest. During her teen years, she divided her time between living in
her divorced parents' unstable, abusive homes and living on the streets. At
age 15, McGowan emancipated herself and moved to Los Angeles to pursue
modeling and acting.

After a series of bit parts, McGowan landed her first major role in the
1992 comedy film *Encino Man*. Her breakthrough came four years later,
when she played Tatum Riley in the hit 1996 slasher-horror movie *Scream*.
McGowan is also known for her portrayal of Paige Matthews, one of a trio of
modern-day witches who use their powers for good, in the popular teen-
oriented television drama *Charmed*. She joined the cast in 2001 and continued in the role until the series ended in 2006.

During her acting career, McGowan frequently spoke out on issues that
mattered to her. In 2008, for instance, she actively opposed Proposition 8,
a California ballot proposal that would have banned gay marriage in the
state. McGowan launched her campaign against misogyny in the entertainment industry in 2015, when she received a film script for an Adam Sandler

movie. A note attached to the script said that any actress interested in auditioning must wear form-fitting jeans or leggings and a low-cut tank top that showed off her cleavage. McGowan expressed her disgust on Twitter, saying that she found the note offensive and resented the casual sexism that pervaded the film industry.

McGowan's stand aroused controversy, especially after she appeared on television talk shows to denounce "the systemic abuse of women in Hollywood." When her agent dropped her, McGowan reassessed her 25-year career and decided to quit acting. "I just hated every part of the system I was in," she recalled. "It was like an alarm bell going off in my head: 'Wake up: this life is not right for you.' And it was like a thunderbolt" (Saner 2018). McGowan announced that she intended to focus her energy on writing, directing, and advocating for women's rights. She also shaved off her long hair to symbolize her rejection of Hollywood's expectations for women.

On October 5, 2017, the *New York Times* published an article alleging that Hollywood film mogul Harvey Weinstein subjected aspiring actresses to sexual harassment and abuse for decades. Investigative reporters uncovered evidence suggesting that the powerful producer paid financial settlements to at least eight actresses to avoid litigation surrounding accusations of sexual misconduct, including a payment of $100,000 to McGowan. Although Weinstein acknowledged behaving inappropriately toward some women, he denied engaging in any nonconsensual sexual activity.

McGowan initially declined to comment on the article, citing a nondisclosure agreement. On October 12, however, she released a series of tweets accusing Weinstein of raping her in a hotel room at the Sundance Film Festival in 1997. She also claimed that many prominent men in the film industry knew about her experience with Weinstein and kept quiet about it. In the midst of her disclosures, Twitter temporarily suspended McGowan's account, claiming that she violated its privacy policy by including a private phone number in a tweet. McGowan's supporters organized a boycott to protest Twitter's actions, which they viewed as an attempt to silence her.

Following McGowan's allegations, many other female celebrities came forward to accuse Weinstein or other prominent men of sexual misconduct. McGowan thus emerged as a key figure in the #MeToo movement, a social media campaign initiated by her former *Charmed* costar, Alyssa Milano, that encouraged millions of women around the world to share their personal stories of sexual harassment or abuse. On October 27, McGowan promoted the movement in a passionate speech at the Women's Convention in Detroit, Michigan. "I have been silenced for 20 years. I have been slut-shamed. I have been harassed. I've been maligned," she declared. "And you know what? I'm just like you. Because what happened to me behind the scenes happens to all of us in this society, and that cannot stand and it will not stand" (McNary 2017).

McGowan adopted a more militant stance than most other #MeToo activists, which complicated her relationship with Milano and some other celebrities involved in the movement. She dismissed the celebrities who wore black to the 2018 Golden Globe Awards, for instance, tweeting that "not one of those fancy people wearing black to honor our rapes would have lifted a finger" if she and other survivors had not come forward (Saner 2018). In January 2018, McGowan released *Brave*, a memoir that covers her early life, her acting career, and her alleged assault by Weinstein. She also appeared in *Citizen Rose* (2018), a documentary television series about her feminist activism. Finally, McGowan launched the #RoseArmy hashtag for people who share her commitment to ending sexism. "I want to dismantle the status quo and I want to shatter the patriarchy," she stated. "It is not working for society, and it is especially not working for women. I want us to be equal. I will not rest until it is so. I believe an *army of thought* will bring about the systemic change we so need. And it starts with us" (Tamblyn 2017).

Further Reading

McGowan, Rose. 2018. *Brave*. New York: HarperCollins.

McNary, Dave. 2017. "Rose McGowan Speaks Out on Sexual Abuse." *Variety*, October 27. https://variety.com/2017/film/news/rose-mcgowan-sexual -abuse-speech-womens-convention-1202600989/

Saner, Emine. 2018. "Rose McGowan: 'Hollywood Is Built on Sickness. It Operates like a Cult.'" *Guardian*, June 1. https://www.theguardian.com/film/2018/ jun/01/rose-mcgowan-interview-hollywood-is-built-on-sickness-it-operates -like-a-cult

Tamblyn, Amber. 2017. "Rose the Riveting." *Bust*, December. https://bust.com/ entertainment/18988-rose-mcgowan-interview.html

Alyssa Milano (1972–)

Actress and activist whose tweet popularized the #MeToo hashtag

Alyssa Jayne Milano was born on December 19, 1972, in the Benson-hurst neighborhood of Brooklyn, New York. She was the oldest of two children born to Thomas Milano, a film music editor, and Lin Milano, a fashion designer. Milano began acting at the age of eight, after a babysitter took her to an open audition for the Broadway musical *Annie* without her parents' knowledge and she won a role as an orphan over 1,500 other children. Milano loved performing and grew determined to make acting her career. Her portrayal of Tony Danza's outspoken daughter Samantha on the popular sitcom *Who's the Boss?* (1984–1992) made her a teen idol during the 1980s. She gained a new generation of fans as Phoebe Halliwell in *Charmed* (1998–2006), a hit fantasy-drama series about three modern-day witches who use their powers for good.

Milano's involvement in social activism began at the onset of the AIDS epidemic, when she met Ryan White (1971–1990), a young man who contracted HIV from a contaminated blood transfusion when he was 13 years old. Due to the fear and stigma surrounding the disease, White's middle school in Indiana refused to allow him to attend classes. Hoping to raise awareness and correct misinformation, Milano agreed to appear with White on *The Phil Donahue Show*. She shocked many viewers by leaning over and kissing him on the cheek to show that the virus could not be transmitted through casual contact. Although White died of AIDS a few years later, he made an indelible impact on Milano's life. "He taught me that I had a power as a celebrity to change things and to stand up for what's right, and he gave me the courage to do that," she stated. "My activism today is a direct reflection of that little boy" (Chuck 2017).

Another formative experience for Milano came in the early 2000s, when she spent three months helping to alleviate poverty in South Africa. She later served as a United Nations International Children's Emergency Fund (UNICEF) ambassador and raised money to provide clean water for people in developing countries through Charity: Water. With the emergence of social media, Milano took full advantage of the platform to educate her fans about social and political causes that mattered to her. During the 2016 presidential campaign, she vocally supported Democratic candidates Bernie Sanders and Hillary Clinton and opposed Republican candidate Donald Trump. After Trump became president, she emerged as a frequent critic of his administration and policies on Twitter.

In October 2017, a series of famous women came forward to accuse Hollywood film producer Harvey Weinstein of sexual misconduct, including Milano's *Charmed* costar Rose McGowan. Milano, who described her own experiences of sexual harassment in the entertainment industry as "too many to count" (Birnbaum 2017), responded by posting a message on Twitter: "If you've been sexually harassed or assaulted, write 'Me Too' as a reply to this tweet." Within 24 hours, 500,000 people responded on Twitter, including dozens of celebrities, and the hashtag #MeToo appeared on Facebook 12 million times (CBS 2017). Although civil rights activist Tarana Burke coined the term "Me Too" prior to the widespread adoption of social media, Milano's tweet turned it into a rallying cry for women around the world and launched a powerful movement aimed at supporting survivors of sexual misconduct.

By demonstrating the magnitude of the problem, Milano hoped to build a community of survivors and create an environment where victims felt empowered to come forward. "We've been hearing a lot about those who caused this kind of hurt and heartache and not enough about the victims who have to overcome and heal. I feel like to be able to do that, you have to know you're part of a community that can support and stand beside you," she stated. "This is not just a Hollywood issue. This happens every day. This happens everywhere. I'm hoping that by putting this focus on giving the power back to the victims, more women can move forward and won't be shamed or blamed. Predators will realize they won't be able to get away with it anymore" (Birnbaum 2017).

In addition to acting and activism, Milano's interests include fashion design. She launched a line of women's clothing aimed at sports fans, called Touch by Alyssa Milano, and promoted it on her Major League Baseball blog. She also appeared as a host and judge on the fashion design competition *Project Runway: All Stars*. Milano married David Bugliari in 2009. They have two children, Milo and Elizabella. After becoming a mother, Milano extended her online activism to include increasing accommodations for breastfeeding in public and improving the diagnosis and treatment of postpartum depression and anxiety.

Further Reading

Birnbaum, Debra. 2017. "Alyssa Milano on #MeToo Campaign: 'I Wanted to Take the Focus Off the Predator.'" *Variety*, October 17. https://variety.com /2017/biz/news/metoo-alyssa-milano-harvey-weinstein-1202592308/

CBS Interactive. 2017. "More Than 12 Million 'Me Too' Facebook Posts, Comments, Reactions in 24 Hours." CBS News, October 17. https://www.cbsnews.com/ news/metoo-more-than-12-million-facebook-posts-comments-reactions-24 -hours/

Chuck, Elizabeth. 2017. "Before #MeToo, before Doug Jones, Alyssa Milano's Activism Started with a Kiss on TV." NBC News, December 16. https:// www.nbcnews.com/news/us-news/metoo-doug-jones-alyssa-milano-s -activism-started-kiss-tv-n829466

Sayej, Nadja. 2017. "Alyssa Milano on the #MeToo Movement: 'We're Not Going to Stand for It Anymore.'" *Guardian*, December 1. https://www .theguardian.com/culture/2017/dec/01/alyssa-milano-mee-too-sexual -harassment-abuse

Mónica Ramírez (1977?–)

Civil rights attorney and activist whose letter sparked the Time's Up movement

Mónica Ramírez was born around 1977 in Fremont, Ohio, a rural community along the Sandusky River. Her family arrived in the area as migrant farmworkers and managed to put down roots before she was born. Although her father worked in manufacturing during her youth, Ramírez heard stories about farming from her parents, grandparents, and the migrant workers who continued to pass through her community every year. Some of these stories focused on the hardships and mistreatment that many agricultural workers endured. Under the guidance of her parents, Ramírez grew determined to fight for social justice for farmworkers. "Many of my family members spent years toiling in the agricultural fields of our nation to, literally, feed our nation," she stated. "My ... parents' influence has helped me to never forget my duty to fight for justice and to work to improve work conditions for farmworkers and all workers in our country" (Valletta 2018).

Ramírez's activism began when she was 14 years old. After the local paper published a notice welcoming the fishermen who arrived in Fremont for the season, she contacted the editor to demand that the paper also recognize the arrival of migrant farmworkers. She ended up serving as a contributing writer focusing on issues affecting farmworkers and the town's Latino residents. During her late teens, Ramírez visited migrant families in the fields through her church and served as a volunteer teacher of migrant children. For a brief period, she worked in the fields picking cucumbers. "I didn't feel that I could properly advocate for farmworkers if I didn't know what it felt like to work in the fields," she said (Best 2018). In 1999, Ramírez earned a degree in communications from Loyola University in Chicago. She went on to earn a law degree from the Ohio State University in 2003, and she later added a master's degree in public administration from Harvard University's Kennedy School of Government.

In 2006, Ramírez joined the Southern Poverty Law Center as a civil rights attorney and launched Esperanza: The Immigrant Women's Legal Initiative. In 2009, Esperanza introduced the Bandana Project, which asked women across the country to decorate and display bandanas to express solidarity with agricultural workers who experienced sexual exploitation. "Farmworker women have reported out at much higher rates of sexual harassment than any other group of women workers in our nation," Ramírez explained. "And that is because the perpetrators believe that no one sees them, no one hears them, no one cares about them, and no one is ever going to do anything to help them" (Fitzpatrick 2018). Ramírez noted that many female farmworkers wore bandanas and loose-fitting clothing to disguise their gender and reduce their vulnerability to sexual harassment.

In 2011, Ramírez cofounded the Alianza Nacional de Campesinas (National Farmworker Women's Alliance), a social justice organization that advocates for immigration, education, and employment policies favorable to female agricultural workers. Its 700,000 members include current and former farmworkers as well as women from farming families. "Part of our work as an organization is to fight for gender equality along all lines," Ramírez said. "So we fight for equal pay, we fight against sexual harassment, we fight for equity. So every person's voice will be valued—everyone will have the opportunity to reach their full potential" (Tang and Feller 2018). With Ramírez serving as president of the board of directors, the organization waged its battle against workplace sexual harassment outside of the public eye for several years. In October 2017, however, a series of female celebrities came forward to accuse Hollywood film producer Harvey Weinstein of sexual misconduct. Their disclosures helped launch the #MeToo movement, a social media campaign aimed at raising awareness of the pervasiveness of sexual harassment.

Ramírez responded to the Weinstein scandal and #MeToo revelations by writing an open letter on behalf of her organization that appeared in *Time* magazine in November 2017. She declared that the Campesinas stood in solidarity with the women of Hollywood. "Even though we work in very different environments, we share a common experience of being preyed upon by individuals who have the power to hire, fire, blacklist and otherwise threaten our economic, physical and emotional security," the letter stated (Best 2018). Around the time Ramírez's letter appeared, a group of powerful women in the entertainment industry launched the Time's Up movement to address gender inequality and power imbalances in the workplace that contribute to harassment behavior. Her letter convinced the Time's Up founders to expand their focus to include working women from marginalized groups. They created the Time's Up Legal Defense Fund to provide legal and financial support to victims of sexual harassment who could not afford it on their own. The initiative raised $20 million within a matter of months (Fitzpatrick 2018).

In January 2018, many people in the entertainment industry promoted the Time's Up movement by wearing black to the Golden Globe Awards. Several celebrities took the initiative a step further by inviting activists to attend the ceremony as their guests. Ramírez walked the red carpet with actress Laura Dern and took advantage of the opportunity to discuss the concerns of farmworker women. In March 2018, Ramírez spoke at the

United Nations to mark International Women's Day. "I feel like everything that has happened over the last few months are not things I ever dreamed of," she acknowledged. "It also really drives home the message that any of us, no matter where we come from, no matter our background, have the ability to make a significant impact. So for little girls who are watching this moment play out, I hope they see they can too" (Best 2018).

Further Reading

Best, Tamara. 2018. "Mónica Ramírez's #MeToo Message for Hollywood, Straight from the Farm." *Daily Beast*, March 9. https://www.thedailybeast.com/monica-ramirezs-metoo-lesson-for-hollywood-straight-from-the-farm

Fitzpatrick, Maya. 2018. "BPR Interviews: Mónica Ramírez." *Brown Political Journal*, April 2. http://www.brownpoliticalreview.org/2018/04/bpr-interviews-Monica-Ramirez/

Tang, Estelle, and Madison Feller. 2018. "Meet the Activists Who Walked the Golden Globes Red Carpet." *Elle*, January 8. https://www.elle.com/culture/movies-tv/g14774201/actress-activist-red-carpet-golden-globes/

Valletta, Lili Gil. 2017. "Meet the Advocate behind the Country's Largest Latina Equal Pay Movement: Mónica Ramírez." *Huffington Post*, October 31. https://www.huffingtonpost.com/entry/meet-Mónica-Ramírez-the-advocate-behind-the-countrys_us_59f8d781e4b0b7f0915f6277

Katie Roiphe (1968–)

Feminist cultural critic known for her controversial views on the #MeToo movement

Katie Roiphe was born on July 13, 1968, to psychoanalyst Herman Roiphe and feminist writer Anne Roiphe. She grew up in New York City and attended the Brearley School, an all-girls, private institution in Manhattan. Roiphe began writing at the age of 12, when severe pneumonia forced her to undergo surgery to remove part of her lung. She spent her convalescence reading nineteenth-century novels and recording her thoughts in a journal. After earning a bachelor's degree from Harvard University-Radcliffe College in 1990, Roiphe went on to complete a doctorate in English Literature at Princeton University in 1996.

Roiphe gained notoriety with the publication of her first book, *The Morning After: Fear, Sex, and Feminism* (1994), a nonfiction examination of growing concerns about date rape on college campuses. Roiphe voiced objections to what she viewed as a cultural expansion of the term "rape." "We all agree that rape is a terrible thing, but we no longer agree on what rape is," she wrote.

"Today's definition has stretched beyond bruises and knives, threats of death or violence to include emotional pressure and the influence of alcohol. The lines between rape and sex begin to blur." Roiphe argued that the expanding definition fed sexual stereotypes and encouraged women to live in perpetual fear of male intentions. She aroused controversy by suggesting that young women should take greater responsibility for their own actions. "If we assume that women are not all helpless and naive, then they should be held responsible for their choice to drink or take drugs," she asserted. "If a woman's 'judgment is impaired' and she has sex, it isn't necessarily always the man's fault; it isn't necessarily always rape" (Roiphe 1993).

Roiphe wrote several more books over the years, including the nonfiction studies *Last Night in Paradise: Sex and Morals at the Century's End* (1997) and *Uncommon Arrangements* (2007), as well as the novel *Still She Haunts Me* (2001). She also contributed numerous essays and book reviews to such publications as *Harper's*, *Slate*, *Vogue*, the *Paris Review*, the *New York Times*, and the *Washington Post*. Roiphe became a professor of journalism at New York University and served as director of the Cultural Reporting and Criticism Program. In 2001, she married attorney Harry Chernoff. They had a daughter together, Violet, and Roiphe also had a son, Leo, as a single mother after they divorced.

In October 2017, dozens of celebrities came forward to accuse Hollywood film mogul Harvey Weinstein of sexual misconduct. These disclosures encouraged millions of women around the world to share their own experiences of sexual harassment and assault online using the hashtag #MeToo. The #MeToo movement generated intense scrutiny of men's behavior toward women in the workplace. Often described as a national reckoning, it produced allegations that led to the downfall of powerful men in many different industries. In this atmosphere of increased awareness and reduced tolerance for sexual harassment, women in the publishing industry circulated an anonymous, crowdsourced document detailing accusations of sexual misconduct—ranging from leering and crude remarks to groping and rape—against more than 70 men. Known as the "S***ty Media Men List," it created a furor in the publishing industry and contributed to a broader debate about the impact of the #MeToo movement.

Roiphe joined this debate by accepting an assignment from the publisher of *Harper's Magazine* to provide a "contrarian" view of the #MeToo movement for publication in the March 2018 issue. Since many women considered Roiphe a divisive figure, her selection to write the cover story aroused controversy—especially when rumors began circulating that her article would publicly identify the creator of the Media Men List. Critics warned that the person in question would likely face career repercussions, online harassment, and physical danger if her identity were revealed. In January 2018, after being contacted by a *Harper's Magazine* fact-checker, writer Moira Donegan preempted the publication of Roiphe's article and came forward as the creator of the list. Roiphe later claimed that she had not planned to mention Donegan's name without her permission.

In her *Harper's Magazine* essay, entitled "The Other Whisper Network," Roiphe claimed that she welcomed the national conversation about sexual harassment that commenced with the #MeToo movement. "I wrote it as a feminist who, of course, shares the goals more broadly of #MeToo," she stated. "Obviously, we all want the men who are abusing power out of power" (Simon 2018). Yet Roiphe also asserted that the voices dominating the #MeToo conversation refused to allow others to express concerns, doubts, or criticism without attacking them. As evidence, she pointed to "the prepublication frenzy of Twitter fantasy and fury" that surrounded her *Harper's Magazine* essay. "Many women still fear varieties of retribution (Twitter rage, damage to their reputations, professional repercussions, and vitriol from friends) for speaking out—this time, from other women," she wrote. "Social media has enabled a more elaborate intolerance of feminist dissenters, as I just personally experienced. Twitter, especially, has energized the angry extremes of feminism.... The vicious energy and ugliness is there beneath the fervor of our new reckoning, adeptly disguised as exhilarating social change" (Roiphe 2018).

Roiphe expressed concerns about how feminist pressure to believe all women who made allegations of sexual harassment created a presumption of guilt and denied men the right to due process. She also questioned whether some inappropriate workplace behaviors—such as touching an employee's back, sending a message the recipient deemed "creepy," or asking for a coworker's phone number—constituted sufficient grounds for ruining a man's career. "If we are going through a true reckoning," she wrote, "there should be space for more authentically diverging points of view, a full range of feelings, space to hash through what is and is not sexual misconduct, which is an important and genuinely confusing question about which reasonable people can and will disagree" (Roiphe 2018).

Roiphe's essay encountered criticism from many #MeToo supporters, who objected to her characterization of them as irrationally angry and vengeful. "Roiphe's piece is part of a larger strain of #MeToo backlash, one that casts survivors and their allies as repressive agents eager to punish anyone with whom they disagree," Anna North wrote in *Vox*. "Public critics of #MeToo have generally received a version of what they doled out: criticism.... Certainly no one deserves harassment or threats, but the idea that the conversation around #MeToo has become prohibitively unsafe for skeptics is not borne out by the evidence" (North 2018).

Further Reading

North, Anna. 2018. "The Controversy around Katie Roiphe's *Harper's* Essay on #MeToo, Explained." *Vox*, April 20. https://www.vox.com/2018/2/5/ 16971286/katie-roiphe-harpers-twitter-moira-donegan-me-too-movement

Roiphe, Katie. 1993. "Date Rape's Other Victim." *New York Times Magazine*, June 13. https://www.nytimes.com/1993/06/13/magazine/date-rape-s -other-victim.html

Roiphe, Katie. 2018. "The Other Whisper Network." *Harper's Magazine*, March. https://harpers.org/archive/2018/03/the-other-whisper-network-2/

Simon, Scott. 2018. "Katie Roiphe on 'The Other Whisper Network.'" NPR, February 10. https://www.npr.org/2018/02/10/584757708/katie-roiphe -on-the-other-whisper-network

Further Resources

The #MeToo Movement

Anderson, Nick. 2018. "Academia's #MeToo Moment: Women Accuse Professors of Sexual Misconduct." *Washington Post*, May 10. https://www .washingtonpost.com/local/education/academias-metoo-moment-women -accuse-professors-of-sexual-misconduct/2018/05/10/474102de-2631 -11e8-874b-d517e912f125_story.html?utm_term=.a04f17eba0e7

Cooney, Samantha. 2017. "These Are the Women Who Have Accused President Trump of Sexual Misconduct." *Time*, December 13. http://time.com/ 5058646/donald-trump-accusers/

Cottle, Michelle. 2018. "Echoes of the Mommy Wars in #MeToo." *Atlantic*, February 11. https://www.theatlantic.com/politics/archive/2018/02/ echoes-of-the-mommy-wars-in-metoo/552830/

Donegan, Moira. 2018. "I Started the Media Men List." *Cut*, January 10. https:// www.thecut.com/2018/01/moira-donegan-i-started-the-media-men-list.html

Gessen, Masha. 2017. "When Does a Watershed Become a Sex Panic?" *New Yorker*, November 14. https://www.newyorker.com/news/our-columnists/when -does-a-watershed-become-a-sex-panic

Gilbert, Sophie. 2017. "The Movement of #MeToo: How a Hashtag Got Its Power." *Atlantic*, October 16. https://www.theatlantic.com/entertainment/archive/ 2017/10/the-movement-of-metoo/542979/

Gray, Emma. 2018. *A Girl's Guide to Joining the Resistance: A Feminist Handbook on Fighting for Good.* New York: HarperCollins.

Kantor, Jodi, and Megan Twohey. 2017. "Harvey Weinstein Paid Off Sexual Harassment Accusers for Decades." *New York Times*, October 5. https:// www.nytimes.com/2017/10/05/us/harvey-weinstein-harassment-allegations .html?_r=0

Kipnis, Laura. 2018. "Has #MeToo Gone Too Far, or Not Far Enough? The Answer Is Both." *Guardian*, January 13. https://www.theguardian.com/commentisfree/ 2018/jan/13/has-me-too-catherine-deneuve-laura-kipnis

MeToo. 2018. https://metoomvmt.org/

New York Times Magazine. 2017. "The Reckoning: Women and Power in the Workplace [interactive online art and essays]." December 13. https://www.nytimes.com/interactive/2017/12/13/magazine/the-reckoning-women-and-power-in-the-workplace.html

North, Anna. 2018. "Celebrities, Politicians, CEOs, and Others Who Have Been Accused of Sexual Misconduct since April 2017." *Vox*, May 25. https://www.vox.com/a/sexual-harassment-assault-allegations-list

Pazzanese, Christina, and Colleen Walsh. 2017. "The Women's Revolt: Why Now, and Where To?" *Harvard Gazette*, December 21. https://news.harvard.edu/gazette/story/2017/12/metoo-surge-could-change-society-in-pivotal-ways-harvard-analysts-say/

Reilly, Katie. 2017. " 'No More.' Read Rose McGowan's First Public Remarks since Accusing Harvey Weinstein of Rape." *Time*, October 27. http://time.com/5000381/rose-mcgowan-harvey-weinstein-speech-transcript/

Roiphe, Katie. 2018. "The Other Whisper Network: How Twitter Feminism Is Bad for Women." *Harper's*, March. https://harpers.org/archive/2018/03/the-other-whisper-network-2/

Solnit, Rebecca. 2018. "Rebecca Solnit on the #MeToo Backlash: Stop Telling Us How to Confront an Epidemic of Violence and Abuse." *Literary Hub*, February 12. https://lithub.com/rebecca-solnit-on-the-metoo-backlash/

Traister, Rebecca. 2017. "Why the Harvey Weinstein Sexual-Harassment Allegations Didn't Come Out Until Now." *Cut*, October 5. https://www.thecut.com/2017/10/why-the-weinstein-sexual-harassment-allegations-came-out-now.html

Traister, Rebecca. 2017. "Your Reckoning. And Mine." *Cut*, November 12. https://www.thecut.com/2017/11/rebecca-traister-on-the-post-weinstein-reckoning.html

Traister, Rebecca. 2018. "No One Is Silencing Katie Roiphe." *Cut*, February 6. https://www.thecut.com/2018/02/rebecca-traister-on-katie-roiphe-harpers-and-metoo.html

Williams, Joan C., and Suzanne Lebsock. 2018. "Now What? Social Media Has Created a Remarkable Moment for Women, but Is This Really the End of Harassment Culture?" *Harvard Business Review*, January. https://hbr.org/cover-story/2018/01/now-what

Zacharek, Stephanie, Eliana Dockterman, and Haley Sweetland Edwards. 2017. "Time Person of the Year: The Silence Breakers." *Time*, December 18. http://time.com/time-person-of-the-year-2017-silence-breakers/

Sexual Harassment and Misogyny in American Society

Amienne, K. A. 2017. "Abusers and Enablers in Faculty Culture." *Chronicle of Higher Education*, November 2. https://www.chronicle.com/article/AbusersEnablers-in/241648?cid=rclink

Anderson, Kristin. 2014. *Modern Misogyny: Anti-Feminism in a Post-Feminine World*. New York: Oxford University Press.

Baker, Carrie. 2008. *The Women's Movement against Sexual Harassment*. New York: Cambridge University Press.

Equal Employment Opportunity Commission (EEOC). 2016. *Report of the Co-Chairs of the Select Task Force on the Study of Sexual Harassment in the Workplace*. June. https://www.eeoc.gov/eeoc/task_force/harassment/upload/report.pdf

Farley, Lin. 1978. *Sexual Shakedown: The Sexual Harassment of Women on the Job*. New York: McGraw-Hill.

Harding, Kate. 2015. *Asking for It: The Alarming Rise of Rape Culture—And What We Can Do about It*. Boston: Da Capo.

Hill, Anita F. 1997. *Speaking Truth to Power*. New York: Doubleday.

Holland, Jack. 2012. *A Brief History of Misogyny: The World's Oldest Prejudice*. New York: Little, Brown.

Kearl, Holly. 2018. *The Facts behind the #MeToo Movement: A National Study on Sexual Harassment and Assault*. Stop Street Harassment, February. http://www.stopstreetharassment.org/wp-content/uploads/2018/01/Full-Report-2018-National-Study-on-Sexual-Harassment-and-Assault.pdf

Kipnis, Laura. 2017. *Unwanted Advances: Sexual Paranoia Comes to Campus*. New York: Harper.

Krakauer, Jon. 2015. *Missoula: Rape and the Justice System in a College Town*. New York: Doubleday.

Lopez, Ricardo. 2017. "Anita Hill on Sexual Harassment: 'Today, More People Would Believe My Story.'" *Variety*, December 8. https://variety.com/2017/biz/news/anita-hill-uta-sexual-harassment-1202634689/

MacKinnon, Catharine A. 1979. *Sexual Harassment of Working Women*. New Haven, CT: Yale University Press.

Mantilla, Karla. 2015. *Gendertrolling: How Misogyny Went Viral*. Santa Barbara, CA: ABC-CLIO.

Mengeling, Michelle A. 2014. "Reporting Sexual Assault in the Military: Who Reports and Why Most Servicewomen Don't." *American Journal of Preventive Medicine* 47(1): 17–25.

Quinn, Zoe. 2017. *Crash Override: How Gamergate (Nearly) Destroyed My Life, and How We Can Win the Fight against Online Hate*. New York: Public Affairs.

Reveal: The Center for Investigative Journalism. 2018. "Rape on the Night Shift: An Investigation into the Sexual Abuse of Immigrant Women in the Janitorial Industry." https://www.revealnews.org/topic/rape-on-the-night-shift/

Senthillingham, Meera. 2017. "Sexual Harassment: How It Stands around the Globe." CNN, November 29. https://www.cnn.com/2017/11/25/health/sexual-harassment-violence-abuse-global-levels/index.html

Solnit, Rebecca. 2017. "The Fall of Harvey Weinstein Should Be a Moment to Challenge Extreme Masculinity." *Guardian*, October 12. https://www.theguardian.com/commentisfree/2017/oct/12/challenge-extreme-masculinity-harvey-weinstein-degrading-women

Stern, Mark Joseph. 2017. "Who's to Blame for America's Sexual Harassment Nightmare? The Supreme Court, for One." *Slate*, October 17. http://www.slate.com/articles/news_and_politics/jurisprudence/2017/10/blame_the_supreme_court_for_america_s_sexual_harassment_nightmare.html

Thomas, Gillian. 2016. *Because of Sex: One Law, Ten Cases, and Fifty Years That Changed American Women's Lives at Work*. New York: St. Martin's Press.

Walton, Gerald. 2017. "What Rape Culture Says about Masculinity." *Conversation*, October 16. https://theconversation.com/what-rape-culture-says-about-masculinity-85513

West, Lindy. 2017. "Brave Enough to Be Angry." *New York Times*, November 8. https://www.nytimes.com/2017/11/08/opinion/anger-women-weinstein-assault.html

Women's Rights and Gender Equality

Adamczyk, Alicia. 2016. "What You Need to Know about Women's Workplace Equality." *Time*, August 26. http://time.com/money/4465918/womens-equality-day/

Adichie, Chimamanda Ngozi. 2015. *We Should All Be Feminists*. New York: Anchor Books.

Grady, Constance. 2018. "The Waves of Feminism, and Why People Keep Fighting over Them, Explained." *Vox*, June 1. https://www.vox.com/2018/3/20/16955588/feminism-waves-explained-first-second-third-fourth

Kimmel, Michael. 2008. *Guyland: The Perilous World Where Boys Become Men*. New York: HarperCollins.

Krause, Alex, and Emily Fetsch. 2016. *Labor after Labor*. Kauffman Foundation Resource Series on Entrepreneurship and Motherhood, May. www.kauffman.org/~/media/kauffman_org/research%20reports%20and%20covers/2016/labor_after_labor_may3b.pdf

LeanIn.Org and McKinsey and Co. 2017. *Women in the Workplace: 2017*. https://womenintheworkplace.com/Women_in_the_Workplace_2017.pdf

Lipman, Joanne. 2018. *That's What She Said: What Men Need to Know (and Women Need to Tell Them) about Working Together*. New York: William Morrow/HarperCollins.

Maclean, Nancy. 2009. *The American Women's Movement, 1945–2000: A Brief History with Documents*. New York: Bedford/St. Martin's.

McGuire, Daniel L. 2010. *At the Dark End of the Street: Black Women, Rape, and Resistance: A New History of the Civil Rights Movement from Rosa Parks to the Rise of Black Power*. New York: Knopf.

Morelli, Caitlin, 2015. "Women's Issues in the Obama Era: Expanding Equality and Social Opportunity under the Obama Administration." *Inquiries* 7(2). http://www.inquiriesjournal.com/articles/992/3/womens-issues-in-the-obama-era-expanding-equality-and-social-opportunity-under-the-obama-administration

Obama, Michelle. 2016. "Remarks by the First Lady and Oprah Winfrey in a Conversation at the United State of Women Summit." June 14. Online by Gerhard Peters and John T. Woolley, the American Presidency Project. http://www.presidency.ucsb.edu/ws/?pid=120902

Shehan, Constance L., ed. 2018. *Gender Roles in American Life: A Documentary History of Political, Social, and Economic Changes.* Santa Barbara, CA: ABC-CLIO.

Spruill, Marjorie. 2017. *Divided We Stand: The Battle over Women's Rights and Family Values That Polarized American Politics.* New York: Bloomsbury.

Tarrant, Shira, ed. 2015. *Gender, Sex, and Politics: In the Streets and between the Sheets in the 21st Century.* New York: Routledge.

Traister, Rebecca. 2018. *Good and Mad: The Revolutionary Power of Women's Anger.* New York: Simon and Schuster.

Index

About the Author

Laurie Collier Hillstrom is a freelance writer and editor based in Brighton, Michigan. She has authored more than 40 books in the areas of American history, biography, and current events. Some of her published works include *Black Lives Matter: From a Moment to a Movement*, *Defining Moments: The Constitution and the Bill of Rights*, and *Defining Moments: Roe v. Wade*.